ANIMAL

Jon Bradfield

From a story by Jon Bradfield
and Josh Hepple

Animal was co-produced by Park Theatre and
Hope Mill Theatre and was first performed at
Hope Mill Theatre, Manchester, on 9 March 2023

ANIMAL

David	Christopher John-Slater
Jill	Amy Loughton
Derek/Nuno	Matt Ayleigh
Mani/Michael	Harry Singh
Liam	Joshua Liburd
Rob/Ray/Alan/Dad	William Oxborrow

Writer	Jon Bradfield
Story Originator	Josh Hepple
Director	Bronagh Lagan
Set And Costume Designer	Gregor Donnelly
Video Designer	Matt Powell
Lighting Designer	Derek Anderson
Sound Designer	Julian Starr
Assistant Director	Teenie Macleod
Movement Director	Cathy Waller
Access Consultant	Cathy Waller
Intimacy Director	Robbie Taylor Hunt
Production Manager (Manchester/London)	Ian Taylor (For E-Stage)
Production Manager (Bristol)	Tabitha Piggott (For E-Stage)
Casting Director	Jane Deitch
Assistant Designer	Ryan Webster
Costume Supervisor	Nicole Bowden

Company Stage Manager	Mel Berry
Assistant Stage Manager	Reuben Bojang
Assistant Stage Manager	Elsie O'Rourke

Producer	Daniel Cooper
Assistant Producer	Ellen Harris

Christopher John-Slater
David

Christopher John-Slater started his career in 2009, when he joined the cast of CBBC show, *The Dumping Ground*. He then went on to do a film with Ken Loach, called *Sorry, We Missed You*. Recently he performed at his first theatre gig in *All of Us* at the National Theatre.

Amy Loughton
Jill

Theatre credits include: *Crackers* (Polka Theatre); *Romeo & Juliet* (Southwark Playhouse); *Henry V* & *The Tempest* (Shakespeare Rose Theatre); *Cathy* (Cardboard Citizens); *Dear Uncle* and *Neighbourhood Watch* (Stephen Joseph Theatre); *A View From the Bridge* (Theatre by the Lake); *Peter Pan* (New Vic Theatre); *Women Power & Politics* (Tricycle Theatre); *Nation* (National Theatre) and *Apart from* George (Finborough Theatre).

TV and film credits include: *The Final Countdown* (Channel 4); *Porridge*, *EastEnders*, *Holby*, *Doctors* and *Emma* for the BBC, *Talking to the Dead* (Sky TV) and feature films *Little Kingdom*, *Crowhurst* and *Once Upon a Time in London*.

Matt Ayleigh
Derek/Nuno

Matt's theatre credits include: *Timons of Athens* (National Theatre), *The Boy on the Swing* (Tobacco Factory); *Love for Love* (Bristol Old Vic); *The Railway Children* (King's Cross); *The Importance of being Earnest* (Theatre Clwyd – Wales Theatre Award nomination); *Precious Little Talent* (Orange Tree).

Television credits include: *The Rook*, directed by Kari Skogland and ITV's *Unforgotten*, directed by Andy Wilson. Film credits include: Kenneth Branagh's *Artemis Fowl* (Disney) and Branagh's *All is True* (Sony).

Matt is also Founder and Director of Bigger Pictures Productions, whose award-nominated films include *Beanie*, *Known Unknown* and *Screening*. Most recently, he directed BFI Network's *Baked Beans*, which premiered at Cambridge and Bolton Film Festival.

Matt is the inaugural winner of the Society of London Theatre's Laurence Olivier Bursary.

Harry Singh
Mani/Michael

Theatre credits include: Jalal in '*But I'm a cheerleader the musical*' (Turbine Theatre); *Carousel in concert 2019*; *West End Does*: *Magic of Animation 2* (Cadogan Hall); *One Young World* Opening Ceremony (Royal Albert Hall). Soloist in *Songs From the Shows* (Yvonne Arnaud theatre).

Credits whilst training include: Fleet in *Titanic*, Fakir in *The Secret Garden* and Fabian in *Twelfth Night*.

Joshua Liburd
Liam

Joshua is so excited and grateful to be involved in the telling of this much needed important story.

Joshua most recently finished the US National tour of *The Great Gatsby* as Jay Gatsby.

Other credits include: Malcom in *Macbeth* (US National Tour), Dr Faustus in *Dr Faustus* (Arcola Theatre/Tangle Theatre), CC White *Dreamgirls* (Savoy Theatre, West End), *Motown The Musical* (Shaftesbury Theatre), *The Book of Mormon* (Prince of Wales Theatre), *The Scottsboro Boys* (Young Vic).

William Oxborrow
Rob/Ray/Alan/Dad

Trained at LAMDA. Theatre credits include: *The Madness of George III* (National Theatre); Orpheus in Jean Anouilh's *Eurydice* (Chichester); the title role in *The Picture of Dorian Gray* (Gate Theatre, Dublin); and with the RSC: *Romeo and Juliet*, *Hamlet*, *The Silent Woman* and *A Clockwork Orange*. In the West End: *The Clandestine Marriage* (Queens); *Boyband* (Gielgud); *Glorious*

(Duchess); *Guys and Dolls* (Savoy and Phoenix). Regional work includes: *The Deep Blue Sea* and *Good* (Royal Exchange Manchester); Neil Bartlett's adaptation of *Great Expectations* (Bristol Old Vic); *The Importance of Being Earnest* (Derby Playhouse); *A Voyage Round My Father* (Salisbury Playhouse); *Diary of A Nobody* (The Royal and Derngate Northampton); two open-air Shakespeares for the Ludlow Festival and five for the Northcott Theatre, Exeter. *A Midsummer Night's Dream, As You Like It* (For Shakespeare's Globe).

TV credits include *Holby City*, *Spooks*, *Rosemary and Thyme*, *The Bill*, and *The Mrs Bradley Mysteries*.

Film credits include: *The Juror*, Tim Burton's *Sweeney Todd*, *The Muppets Most Wanted*, *The Anarchists' AGM*, and the forthcoming *Borderland* for Sky Cinema.

Jon Bradfield
Writer

Jon co-wrote and composed the songs for Above The Stag Theatre's popular and critically acclaimed 12-year run of queer adult pantomimes. His other collaborations with Martin Hooper include *Ghosted: Another F***ing Christmas Carol* (The Other Palace Theatre); the musical *He Shoots, He Scores!*, and the play *A Hard Rain*, which was also produced in New York. Their new company, He's Behind You!, will present its first show *Sleeping Beauty Takes A Prick* from November 2023 at the Charing Cross Theatre. Jon wrote *Missing Alice* for BBC4 and the Old Vic, part of Mark Gatiss' *Queers* series, with Rebecca Front as Alice; and the forthcoming TV movie *Romantic Friction*, to be distributed internationally in 2023.

Josh Hepple
Story Originator

Josh Hepple is an activist with severe cerebral palsy. He has a masters in law and teaches at various universities. He has been a theatre reviewer, and is an equality trainer and a writer-journalist at the *Guardian* and *Huffington Post*.

Bronagh Lagan
Director

Originally from Northern Ireland, Bronagh is passionate about directing new writing, particularly from underrepresented communities.

Bronagh's Olivier nominated production of *Cruise* by Jack Holden was the first new play to open the West End after the pandemic. *Cruise* returned to the West End last year for a sold out run at The Apollo Theatre. She also directed a film version of the show in Shoreditch Town Hall's Ditch which won an ONCOMM award for Best Recorded Show.

She has directed a number of productions at both Park Theatre and Hope Mill Theatre, Bronagh's production of *Rags*, the musical by Charles Strouse and Stephen Schwartz at Park Theatre received nine Off West End Theatre Award nominations, including Best Director and Best Production. Bronagh worked closely with Stephen Schwartz in reimagining the script for an actor-musician production and curated a cast album; She also directed the European premiere of *Little Women, the musical* at Park Theatre which is available on Broadway HD.

Bronagh recently directed the UK Regional Touring Production of *The Rise and Fall of Little Voice* starring Christina Bianco, the award nominated *Broken Wings*, musical and *Rumi: The Musical* at The London Coliseum starring Rami Karimloo.

West End credits: *Cruise* (The Apollo Theatre); *Rumi: The Musical* (London Coliseum); *Cruise* (Duchess Theatre); *Umm Kulthum, the Golden Era*

(London Palladium); *Broken Wings* (Theatre Royal Haymarket/ Charing Cross Theatre); *Rags the Musical in Concert* (Lyric Theatre).

Other directing credits: *The Rise and Fall of Little Voice* (UK Regional Tour); *A-Typical Rainbow* (Turbine); *Little Women*; *Rags the Musical* (Park Theatre/Hope Mill Theatre); *Putting It Together* (Hope Mill Theatre, Manchester); *A Christmas Carol* (Ivy Studio); *A Winter's Tale* (Rose Theatre, Kingston); *Brexit, the Musical* (C Venues, Edinburgh); *tick, tick... BOOM!* (Park Theatre); *Promises, Promises* (Southwark Playhouse); *As You Like It* (Jackson's Lane Arts Centre); *James and the Giant Peach* (UK and International Tour); *Portia Coughlan* (The Old Red Lion Theatre); *Girlfriends* (Union Theatre); *Blood Wedding* (Courtyard Theatre); *Henry VI, Part 1* (Rose Theatre); *Julius Caesar* (The Scoop).

Gregor Donnelly
Set and Costume Designer

Gregor trained in Set and Costume design on the final ever Motley Theatre Design Course in 2010 and has designed for theatre, concerts and events all over the UK and abroad.

In 2016 he was nominated for Best Set Design and Best Costume Design, Off West End Awards for the J.B. Priestly play *Benighted* directed by Stephen Whitson. In 2017, he was nominated for Best Costume Design, Off West End Theatre Awards for *The Autumn Garden*, directed by Anthony Biggs. He was also nominated for Best Set Design, Off West End Theatre Awards in 2018 for *Peter Pan* directed by Jonathan O'Boyle and for Best Set Design for *Rags the Musical* (Park Theatre) in 2019, directed by Bronagh Lagan.

Set and Costume credits include: *Broken Wings* (Charing Cross Theatre); *Rumi* (London Coliseum/D'reesha Arts Festival, Qatar); *Stones in his Pockets* (Belfast Lyric); Theatre Café Channel episodes 1-5 (streaming Theatre Channel, UK/Playbill, USA); *Umm Kulthum & the Golden Era* (London Palladium/Dubai Opera House); *Jack and the Blingstalk* (Harold Pinter); *I Loved Lucy* (Arts Theatre/Lucille Lortel Theatre, NYC/Woodstock Theatre, NY); *Cat – the Play!* (Ambassadors Theatre); Media Suite design, Olivier Awards (Royal Albert Hall); *Rags the Musical*, *Snow Queen* and *Peter Pan* (Park Theatre); *The Throne* (Charing Cross Theatre); *The Astonishing Times of Timothy Cratchit* and *Rags* (Hope Mill Theatre); *The Jazz Age* and *Shirley Mander* (Playground Theatre); *Driving Miss Daisy*, *Daddy Long Legs*, *Marry Me A Little*, *Peter Pan* and *Stones in his Pockets* (Barn Theatre, Cirencester); *Me and My Girl* (Frinton Summer Theatre); *My Son Pinocchio* (Southwark Playhouse); *Shirley Valentine* (Byre Theatre); *Damn Yankees* (Unicorn Theatre); *Laughing Matters*, Celia Imrie's one woman show *Crazy Coques*, *The Great British Musicals* (St James Theatre/London Hippodrome); *Dirty Dating* (Stockport Plaza/Epstein Theatre, Liverpool); *Rumpy Pumpy* (Windsor Theatre Royal/Union Theatre).

Concert credits include: Bastille's *'Doom Days'* album launch concert.

Opera credits include: *The Angel Esmeralda* (Silk Street Theatre, GSMD); *Xerxes* and *Turn of the Screw* (Byre Theatre, Scotland/tour); *La Bohème* (Thaxted Theatre); *Barber of Seville* and *La Bohème* (King's Head Theatre) and *A Dinner Engagement* and *Comedy on the Bridge* (Rosemary Branch).

Derek Anderson
Lighting Designer

Lighting Design credits include: *Hound of the Baskervilles*, *Our Man in Havana*, *Our Friends, the Enemy*, *If We Got Some More Cocaine* (UK Tour); *Sweeney Todd* (Duetsches

Theatre Munich); *New Possibilities* (SSE Arena Wembley); *One Flew Over the Cuckoo's Nest, Handbagged* and *Spamalot* (English Theatre Frankfurt); Whatsonstage Awards (Prince of Wales Theatre); *What I Go To School For* (Theatre Royal Brighton); *Rumplestiltskin* (Theatre Royal Bath/ Metropolitan Arts Centre, Belfast); *Sunset Boulevard* (Yvonne Arnaud Theatre); *Pure Imagination, Marry Me a Little*, Andrew Lippa in Concert, *Scenes From a Marriage* (St James Theatre); *Man Up, Ignition* (Frantic Assembly); *Henry V* (Cambridge Arts Theatre); *The Wedding Singer, How To Succeed in Business* (Lowry Theatre); *Dessert, Promises Promises, Allegro, The Grand Hotel, Uppercut, Followers* (Southwark Playhouse); *Rags, My Dad's Gap Year, Hatched and Dispatched* (Park Theatre); *Rags, Putting it Together* (Hope Mill, Manchester); *The Beautiful Game* (Union Theatre); *Wonderful Town* (Arts Ed); *As You Like It*, Musical Theatre and Acting Showcase (Mountview Academy).

As Associate Lighting Designer: *Shakespeare in Love, Henry V* (Noel Coward); *Silver Tassie, Great Britain* (National Theatre); *Le Corsaire* (English National Ballet); *The El Train* (Hoxton Hall); *Birdland* (Royal Court); *Skylight* (Wyndhams Theatre/ Golden Theatre, NY – Winner for Best Lighting Design for the 2015 Tony Awards); *Fatal Attraction* (Theatre Royal Haymarket); *Charlie and the Chocolate Factory* (Theatre Royal, Drury Lane – Olivier Award for Best Lighting 2014).

Julian Starr
Sound Designer

Sound Designer and Composer: Queensland Theatre Company; *Return to the Dirt* (Brisbane Metro Arts); *Elektra/Orestes* – Blue Curtains Best Sound Design 2020 (Belvoir St Theatre); *Miss Peony The Australian Tour* (The Old Fitz Theatre);

Hyperdream – Sydney Theatre Award Best Sound Design (West End); *ZOG* (UK Tour/Park Theatre); *Animal, Rose* – Offie Nominated Best Sound Design, *Never Not Once, Cry Havoc, Martha, Josie* and the *Chinese Elvis* (Park Theatre); *Lesbian Space Crime, You Only Live Forever* (Soho Theatre); *Sleepwalking* (Hampstead Theatre); *Axolotl* (Lithuania Tour); *How To Survive an Apocalypse, Scrounger* – Offie Nominated Best Sound Design, *The Wind of Heaven* (Finborough Theatre); *The Dwarfs* – Offie Nominated Best Sound Design (White Bear); *Aisha* – Offie Nominated Best Sound Design (Tristan Bates Theatre); *Kindred Spirits* – Offie Nominated Best Sound Design, *The Woman Who Amuses Herself* – Offie Nominated Best Sound Design (Brockey Jack Studio); *Horse Play* (Riverside Studio); *Song From Far Away, Not Dying* HOME Manchester.

Events Sound Engineer; The Royal Edinburgh Military Tattoo (Edinburgh Castle).

Site Specific: *The Comedy of Errors, Pericles* (17th Valtice Castle, Czech Republic); Kings Head Theatre 50th Celebration; *The Third* (V&A Museum).

Media: *Fizzy Sherbet Podcast; White Tuesday* (The Sarah Awards New York City Best

Audio Fiction). ABC/BBC/Disney Television Series *Bluey* Music Editor.

Positions: Associate Sound Designer to The Finborough Theatre London.

Touring Sound Engineer to *An Inspector Calls* (UK/Ireland Tour); Sound Engineer Songs For *Nobodies* (West End); Sound Engineer *The Tap Pack* (West End); *Richard III* (Sydney Opera House).

Matt Powell
Video Designer

Matt (they/she/he) is a non-binary video designer, musical theatre director and queer practitioner. Their video design work is contemporary, blending photo-realism, 2D animation, live camera and digital architectures to create 'artfully designed' (The Stage) and reality defying concepts. They are a part time PhD candidate at the University of Wolverhampton exploring producing and developing queer musicals & representation.

Recent Video Design and Digital credits include: *Blow Down* (Leeds Playhouse); *Rumi* (D'asha Performance Arts Festival/London Coliseum); *Accidental Death Of An Anarchist* (Lyric Hammersmith, Sheffield Theatres); *How a City Can Save the World* (Sheffield Theatres); *A-Typical Rainbow* (Turbine Theatre); *Flight* (Royal College of Music); *But What If You Die* (Camden People's Theatre); *Old Friends* (Digital); *Bloody Difficult Women* (Edinburgh Fringe, Riverside Studios); *Santa Must Die* (Alphabetti Theatre); *Snowflake* (The Lowry, Salford Quays); *Watford Big Bunting, Buffergram* (Watford Palace Theatre); *34* (Aria Entertainment/The Lowry); *Public Domain* (ALPMusicals/Vaudeville Theatre/Southwark Playhouse) *The Blazing World* (University of the Arts, Philadelphia); *Wilf Goes Wild* (MPTheatricals); *Shift+Alt+Right* (ALPMusicals); *Queered* (MPTheatricals); *On Hope: A Digital Song Cycle* (The Other Palace); *Plaza* (Royal Central School of Speech and Drama), *American Idiot* (Derby Theatre.)

Recent Directing credits include: *The Unconventionals* (VAULT Festival); *Crazy For You* (Derby Theatre); *Is He Musical* (Curve/The Other Palace).

Teenie Macleod
Assistant Director

Teenie trained at Performing Arts Studio Scotland and Associated Studios.

Credits include: *Broken Wings*, (Assistant Director, Charing Cross Theatre); *Little Women*, (Assistant Director, Park Theatre); *C-O-N-T-A-C-T* (Assistant Director); *Rags: The Musical* (Assistant Choreographer & Children's Director, Park Theatre); *Good Omens*, UK Press Tour (Movement Director, Amazon); *Hansel & Gretel* (Assistant Choreographer, Rose Theatre); *An Evening With Neil Gaiman* (Movement Director, Royal Festival Hall); *Into The Woods* (Assistant Choreographer, Chelsea Theatre); *Everything That Rises Must Dance*, (Complicité); *The Testing Ground* (Dance Captain); *The Lemonade Kid* (Choreographer, Churchill Theatre); *Balletic Bagatelle* (Assistant Choreographer, Hampton Court Playhouse).

Nicole Bowden
Costume Supervisor

Nicole works as a Costume Supervisor and Maker across Theatre, Film and Dance. Supervising credits include: *Ghostbusters: The Gates of Gozer* (Secret Cinema); *On The Ropes* (Park Theatre); *Blood Wedding* (Central School Of Speech and Drama); and *Pinocchio* (Cornerstone Arts Centre. Making credits include: *Heathers* (The Other Palace); *Magic Goes Wrong* (Apollo Theatre); *Dirty Dancing* (The Dominion); and *Magic Mike's Last Dance* (Warner Bros and Mammoth Productions).

Ian Taylor (Estage)
Production Manager (Manchester/London)

Ian Taylor is a Technical and Production Manager with over a decade of experience in the theatre and events industry. Ian has an extensive background in stage management, production management, technical management and as managing director of eStage, a company dedicated to serving the entertainment industry's needs.

In 2012 he started production managing and has worked for Birmingham Rep, Sheffield Theatres,

Bush Theatre, Hampstead Theatre, The Royal Opera, Southwark Playhouse, The Park Theatre, The Philharmonia Orchestra, W11 Opera, Arcola Theatre, Troupe Productions, Papatango and Secret Cinema. In 2021/22, Ian was appointed Technical Manager of Bush Theatre, London before returning to full-time production management under eStage.

Ian has over a decade of expertise in managing OKEDIA eStage's digital services offering and MiniStage, its 3D printing service.

In 2016 Ian founded the Backstage Professional Development Conference launched by the team at eStage to bring together industry professionals offering knowledge, advice, and guidance.

Ian holds a bachelor's degree in stage management and technical theatre, with honours, from the Guildhall School of Music and Drama.

Tabitha Piggott
Production Manager (Bristol)

Tabitha Piggott is a production manager for eStage working in theatre and opera, with a particular passion for new writing. She studied Production and Technical Arts at LAMDA as a Leverhulme Arts Scholar, and was production manager on Papatango and Bush Theatre's Olivier Award winning Old Bridge in 2021.

Credits as Production Manager include: *All of Us, Barrier(s)*, Connections 2022 (National Theatre); *Only an Octave Apart* (Wilton's Music Hall); *Paradise Now!, Favour, Red Pitch, Old Bridge, Overflow* (Bush Theatre); *Winner's Curse, The 4th Country* (Park Theatre); *Faun* (Cardboard Citizens); *The Boys are Kissing, Moreno* (Theatre503); *Fefu and her Friends* (Tobacco Factory Theatres); *The Dancing Master* (Buxton Opera House).

As Assistant Production Manager: *The Pillowman* (West End); *Raising Icarus* (Birmingham Rep).

Mel Berry
Company Stage Manager

Melissa graduated with a degree in Theatre Production (Arts and Stage Management) from Winchester University in 2015. Since then, she has stage managed over fifty shows and these include: *The View From Nowhere, Black Chiffon, Corpse!* and *King Hamlin* (Park Theatre); *The Silence of Snow* (Leicester Square Theatre); *Mad As Hell* (Jermyn Street Theatre); *Lord Of The Flies* (Greenwich Theatre); *Daisy Pulls It Off* (Charring Cross Theatre); *Cuckoo* (Soho Theatre); *Robin Hood* (Salisbury Playhouse).

Reuben Bojang
Assistant Stage Manager and AV Op

Reuben is a stage manager from North London. After completing his Production Arts training, Reuben began his career as a freelance sound technician before making his transition to the theatre world.

Theatre credits include: *Pals* (Tabard Theatre); *Romeo and Juliet* (Tabard Theatre); *Henry V – Lion Of England* (Edinburgh Fringe); *Hamlet – Horatio's Tale* (Edinburgh Fringe); *A Walk to Jerusalem* (regional tour); *The Marilyn Conspiracy* (Edinburgh Fringe); *Under Milk Wood* (Filodrammatici Theatre Milan/ regional tour); *A Christmas Carol* (Teatro Litta Milan/Regional tour/Edinburgh Fringe); *Snatched!* (White Bear Theatre); *9 Circles* (Park Theatre/Edinburgh Fringe); *Make Mine A Double Season* (Park Theatre); *Pickle* (Park Theatre/Radlett Centre); *Picasso* (Playground Theatre); *Right Dishonournable Friend* (VAULT Festival).

PARK THEATRE

Park Theatre was founded by Artistic Director, Jez Bond and Creative Director Emeritus, Melli Marie. The building opened in May 2013 and, with eight West End transfers, two National Theatre transfers and 13 national tours in its first ten years, quickly garnered a reputation as a key player in the London theatrical scene. Park Theatre has received six Olivier nominations, won numerous Off West End Offie Awards, and won The Stage's Fringe Theatre of the Year and Accessible Theatre Award.

Park Theatre is an inviting and accessible venue, delivering work of exceptional calibre in the heart of Finsbury Park. We work with writers, directors and designers of the highest quality to present compelling, exciting and beautifully told stories across our two intimate spaces.

Our programme encompasses a broad range of work from classics to revivals with a healthy dose of new writing, producing in-house as well as working in partnership with emerging and established producers. We strive to play our part within the UK's theatre ecology by offering mentoring, support and opportunities to artists and producers within a professional theatre-making environment.

Our Creative Learning strategy seeks to widen the number and range of people who participate in theatre, and provides opportunities for those with little or no prior contact with the arts.

In everything we do we aim to be warm and inclusive; a safe, welcoming and wonderful space in which to work, create and visit.

★ ★ ★ ★ ★ "A five-star neighbourhood theatre." Independent

As a registered charity [number 1137223] with no public subsidy, we rely on the kind support of our donors and volunteers. To find out how you can get involved visit parktheatre.co.uk

For Park Theatre

Artistic Director
Jez Bond

Executive Director
Vicky Hawkins

Creative Learning

Community Engagement Manager
Nina Graveney-Edwards

Creative Learning Leaders
Amy Allen, Josh Picton, Kieran Rose, Vanessa Sampson

Development

Development Director
Tania Dunn

Development & Producing Assistant
Ellen Harris

HOPE MILL THEATRE

The award-winning Hope Mill Theatre was the dream of couple Joseph Houston and William Whelton, who, after a career in Musical Theatre and living in London, became inspired by the highly regarded off-West End theatres and the high-quality work they were producing. With the growing theatre industry blossoming in Manchester and no medium-sized venues producing musicals, they set up and established the independent venue in November 2015.

The venue has firmly placed itself on the northern map for its ambitious in-house musical productions, which include Parade, Hair - the Musical (London, UK Tour); the UK premiere of Yank! (Charing Cross Theatre, London); the European premiere of Little Women, Spring Awakening, Pippin (Southwark Playhouse, London); Aspects of Love (Southwark Playhouse); The Return of the Soldier, Putting It Together, Rags (Park Theatre), Mame (starring Tracie Bennett), the world premiere of the new musical The Astonishing Times of Timothy Cratchit, Jonathan Harvey's, Hushabye Mountain and new play CLASSIC! (Edinburgh Fringe Festival).

Their 2021 revival of RENT received rave reviews from critics and audiences alike and won WhatsOnStage Award for Best Regional Production and Best Production at the Manchester Culture Awards. Their recent revival of The Wiz also received critical acclaim.

In October 2016, Joseph and William were awarded the Hospital Club Award for their contribution to theatre and performance. In 2017, they picked up a Special Achievement Award at the Manchester Theatre Awards. The venue was nominated for the Peter Brook Empty Space Award, won a Northern Soul Award for small theatre of the year, and won the prestigious The Stage Fringe Theatre of the Year Award in 2018. The venue was also awarded the WhatsOnStage Awards' WhatsOffStage Award for Best Front of House Team and Favourite Theatre in 2018. They were also nominated for a Manchester City Council Culture Award for Outstanding Contribution and have been nominated for The Manchester Peoples Culture Award.

Joseph and William joined forces with Aria Entertainment to spearhead the venue as a regional home for new musicals and musical revivals, and their successful collaboration saw them named on The Stage 100 list in 2018/19 and 2019/20. Joseph and William were also featured on the Stage 100 again in 2021, recognising those in the industry who made an important amount of work and positive impact during the pandemic. William Whelton is a recipient of the Stage One Young Producers bursary.

In 2019 the venue transitioned into a charity – A Factory of Creativity CIO – allowing them to continue their extraordinary work, including the creation of Hope Mill Theatre School, a community hub for residents and artists, which is also home to their community choir, amateur dramatics company, and youth outreach programmes.

In addition to the creative output of the venue, from both in-house and received productions, the charity works tirelessly to provide opportunities to members of their community, through their ticket initiatives, scholarship funding and providing platforms for emerging artists.

To find out more information on how you can support Hope Mill Theatre in their exciting ventures please visit: **hopemilltheatre.co.uk**.
Hope Mill Theatre's registered charity number is: 1183251

Twitter: **@Hopemilltheatr1**
Facebook & Instagram: **Hope Mill Theatre**

ANIMAL

Jon Bradfield

From a story by Jon Bradfield and Josh Hepple

Introductions

I was a reviewer at the Edinburgh Festival Fringe for a number of years, and I always had the idea that I wanted to write something on disability and sexuality from a semi-autobiographical perspective. I would always give this ambition everything I had for the two weeks after the Fringe, but would quickly be consumed by law school starting again at the end of September.

During the Christmas period of 2014, I went to see a pantomime version of *Treasure Island* with a group of friends at Above the Stag Theatre in Vauxhall, London. I naively thought that it would be a children's panto, so was startled to find myself in an audience of gay men. I loved the show. Despite having been a reviewer for many years, I had never seen comedy which chimed with my own sense of humour as well as this pantomime did. I went back to the annual panto each Christmas, whilst also working at the Edinburgh Fringe in various capacities every August. The idea for my own play was becoming stronger and stronger, but I had no experience as a writer and the hours I was putting into the writing felt futile and unproductive. I had many other things I could get on with, where I knew what I was doing.

With absolutely no expectations, I reached out to Jon Bradfield, the co-writer of the pantos I kept returning to and enjoying so much, and asked him to have a look at what I had written. Naturally, there was no funding available for Jon, no official commission, so I knew that I had contacted him on a whim – but the more that we spoke, Jon began to seriously consider taking on this project as a writer.

It was the start of a very close friendship, and I enjoyed how curious Jon became about certain parts of my life. I had already written quite openly in the *Guardian* about sex, so I was used to being quite public about my intimate life. I spent lots of time with Jon talking about different ideas and experiences I had. Jon did a fantastic job at keeping my ideas authentic while creating a fictional narrative. We created a semi-autobiographical character, David, and we made every effort to ensure that he was not any type of angelic saint or victim, but a character who had the ability to love and hurt others while having cerebral palsy.

It has been amazing to work with Jon. I made sure to grant him the creative freedom he asked for and was grateful that he would always check with me to see that what he'd written was authentic and reflected the ideas I wanted to convey. It is not a surprise that *Animal* has expanded dramatically from my initial starting points, but the story Jon tells is better, thanks to which those ideas are explored in a more beautiful and artistic way.

Thanks to everyone who has been involved in bringing this play to the stage, especially Daniel Cooper and Bronagh Lagan. I want to dedicate this to Jonathan Cooper who I miss every day. We became very good friends after working together for ten years as lawyers on criminalisation of same-sex activity. Jonathan encouraged me to talk about sexuality and use it to create empathy and change. Jonathan, I'm sorry you won't get to see it. You were right, I have no desire to become a nun and do not regret anything you encouraged me to do.

Thanks also to all those wonderful men who I have met. No conversation in *Animal* is based on a real conversation and no character is based on any real individual.

Josh Hepple

Commissioners, look away now: I'm not great at big ideas. Perhaps it's why I've adapted so many fairytales. So to have Josh bring me such an eye-opening suggestion – and to trust me with such a personal project – was a gift. I'd never have thought of writing about a man who can't wank, nor would I have felt entitled to, but I was instantly smitten. After all, a protagonist needs both a desire and an obstacle, and here were both, entwined.

Neither of us wanted our play to be 'about disabled people', plural. That wouldn't be a project for me to write, and I was glad to stick to the tantalising brief: to tell a story about wanking, and sex, and reliance. The play – *Animal* – isn't activism, and it isn't agitprop. Like most plays, it asks for nothing but your empathy. But Josh's act of willing *Animal* into existence *is* a kind of activism. It's saying that someone 'like' David is worth our time and attention; worthy of being centre stage as the complex, unique central character in a play, representative of nobody and yet – I hope – relatable in some ways to anyone reading or watching the play. When discussing the play recently, Josh said eloquently that giving and receiving sex, love and affection – and being *seen* as deserving of them – are a big part of the human experience. Take that away, and you take away a part of someone's humanity.

Before I wrote a single word I spent a lot of time getting to know Josh, discussing his initial ideas (which kick the play off and resurface at a number of important moments), as well as his philosophy about disability and the practicalities of his life as someone who relies on people almost round-the-clock for essential things that many of us take for granted – and how that intersects with having a sex life.

As Josh says, he was excited by the idea that a play about sex and disability could have some of the comic spirit, unabashed humour, open-hearted warmth and big characterisations that he'd seen in the adult pantomimes I had co-written with Martin Hooper. But he was clear that the humour mustn't be at the expense of disability; that we shouldn't invite people to laugh at impairments to make them palatable, even if our central character's insecurities mean he is sometimes painfully self-deprecating.

David's impairments and practical circumstances are similar to Josh's, and a few moments in the play are inspired by moments in his life. But David isn't Josh, and couldn't be. Character is born of story and action, and this story is a fiction. From the start, I was determined that to whatever degree *Animal* was rooted in the specifics of someone's life, it should stand as a piece of drama in its own right. I wanted the freedom to throw characters at each other, each with their own conflicting needs, and see what I could grow from that – writing being, at least in the first place, improvisation. I thought the subject deserved that, and that I did too. I wanted to write a play with a satisfying shape, with a beginning, middle and end. Life isn't like that.

(It's worth noting that, for simplicity, in some ways I've given David an easier ride than he might have 'in real life'. Arranging the care he relies on – employing personal assistants, engaging agencies or asking friends for help – can be a Sisyphean task. A lack of money and an apparent dearth of casual workers mean that, on a bad week, almost all of David's energy might be spent on the vital but dehumanisingly boring task of ensuring he'll be able to eat, drink and go to the toilet tomorrow.)

Of course, the play isn't only a reflection of Josh's experience of the world. It's informed by my own perspective of becoming friends and collaborators with someone with severe impairments. All of which makes this a deeply *weird* experience for him. After all, here is a character who inhabits a body like his and a world like his, but who wilfully speaks and acts differently to him. Here are experiences – however fictionalised – that are immediately familiar to him, but which pepper a narrative he hasn't lived. Here are characters – an assistant, a housemate, lovers – who fulfil roles that people in his own life have occupied, but who refuse to behave like them. It must feel simultaneously exposing and erasing. For his willingness to go on that journey, for his bravery, for his ability to push me further, and for his frequent and often creative insight, I'm grateful.

For Josh's part, I think there's something very cool about someone who loves theatre, but who is neither a writer nor a producer, nevertheless manifesting a play by persuading someone to write it. Josh is a persuasive guy. He has to be. He's used to recruiting people, formally and informally, to make things possible that he can't do by himself. Perhaps this play is an extreme example of that. We talk a lot about access in theatre, but real access is complicated and requires flexibility. Theatre has very prescriptive roles and established ways of doing things. Josh isn't a writer, or a producer, or a director, and yet with *Animal* he has been, in a unique and valid way, a theatre-maker.

In praise of prizes: You're watching or reading *Animal* thanks to the Hope Mill Theatre's Through the Mill Playwriting Prize, created in association with Jonathan Harvey. This is possibly the sort of thing one shouldn't say publicly, but the truth is, by the time it won the award, *Animal* had been submitted without success to pretty much every funded theatre or company producing new writing that you can think of. That's not an anomaly – few new plays begin their journey to production by landing unsolicited in a theatre's inbox. But prizes, unlike theatres, are free to assess plays on their own terms, outside of such considerations as: Is it affordable? Will it sell? Who is the writer? Does it fit within our programme? Even if you don't win, they'll often give you helpful feedback (thanks Papatango team!). If you're a playwright – or trying to be: look for writing prizes, make their deadlines *your* deadlines, and submit.

Thank you: I'm grateful to the following, whose thoughtful and expert feedback has helped shape this script: Matt Applewhite, Daniel Cooper, my kind, patient and hilarious agent Alec Drysdale, Jonathan Harvey, Laura Klimke, Bronagh Lagan, Noemi Spanos and Daniel Raggett.

Jon Bradfield

Characters

DAVID, *twenty-five. David has cerebral palsy. He uses a powered wheelchair, he has a speech impairment, and he has uncontrollable bodily movements. He can type with his fingers on a phone but cannot use a pen or hold a pint*
JILL, *thirties or so*
DEREK, *thirties*
MANI, *twenties, British Asian. Dresses playfully*
LIAM, *twenties. Muscular build*
MICHAEL, *early twenties*
DAD, *fifties*

Hook-ups:
ROB
RAY
NUNO
ALAN

HELPLINE ADVISER (*voice only*)

Suggested Doubling

The actor playing Mani can play Michael; the actor playing Derek can play Nuno; the actor playing Dad can play Rob, Ray and Alan. If the adviser's dialogue is live rather than recorded, she can be voiced by the actor playing Jill.

Setting

The play starts in winter and ends in late summer. Most scenes take place in David's two-bedroom, ground-floor flat, in his living room or bedroom. The final scene is set in his garden.

Performance Notes

Scene titles in the script are not intended to be displayed.

Text conversations and dating app messages (indented in the script) could be displayed, or be spoken – live or recorded – or both. But they sometimes serve the practical purpose of allowing for scene transitions, especially for the actor playing David. The hook-up chats we see onscreen could look like Grindr, or a fictional dating/hook-up app.

David's speech impairment, and how consistently other characters understand him, may depend on the actor playing David and what feels comfortable. The company can experiment with how often characters might need David to repeat himself: it may be more than indicated, but again this should be decided in collaboration with the actor playing David. If specific words in David's lines are particularly challenging for the actor to articulate, judicious alternatives may be substituted.

David has involuntary physical reactions to anxiety and excitement, a manifestation of his cerebral palsy. The specifics of this may be explored and experimented with by the actor in rehearsal.

It should be possible to stage sex scenes as written without showing full nudity, with smart use of angles and furniture and a bit of inventive duvet work!

This text went to press before the end of rehearsals and so may differ slightly from the play as performed.

Scene: David vs the Autosuck

DAVID*'s living room, late afternoon or early evening.*

A small ground-floor flat, level access throughout. In the room: desk and computer. TV. Sofa, perhaps it's a sofa-bed. Door out to hallway. Another door to a small kitchen. Window to garden or street. A movie poster on the wall: Call Me By Your Name, *perhaps.*

DAVID *sits in his wheelchair. On the desk next to him is the 'Autosuck' sex toy, though we needn't notice it at first, or realise what it is. He's on hold on his phone which is nestled between his thighs on the seat of the wheelchair. It's on speakerphone. The hold music is classical and a message plays on loop: 'Thank you for holding. We'll connect you to the next available operator. Calls are recorded for training purposes.'*

The call connects. A female adviser answers.

ADVISER. Thanks for holding. How can I help you?

  DAVID*'s voice is quite difficult to tune into.*

DAVID. I ordered something from you but I'm having problems with it.

ADVISER. Sorry – the line went funny, would you mind saying that again?

DAVID (*trying to speak more clearly*). I. Ordered. Something. From –

ADVISER. You ordered something, what did you order?

  A slight pause of embarrassment.

DAVID. The Autosuck.

ADVISER. I think I'm going deaf here! Once more?

DAVID. The Aut-o-suck!

ADVISER. That's better! The Autosuck. Yes.

DAVID. I'm having problems with it.

ADVISER. Problems, was that?

DAVID. Yeah.

ADVISER. Right lovely, let me just... What seems to be the problem?

DAVID. I can't use it.

ADVISER. Okay...

DAVID. I can't get my penis into it.

ADVISER. You can't get your... (*With a weary sigh.*) Oh I see. Well if it's really that big you should probably see a doctor. Sober up, sir, goodbye.

The line goes dead.

DAVID. Wait! Fuck.

From the kitchen we hear:

DEREK (*off*). Did you say something, buddy?

DAVID. No.

DAVID *redials. Hold music again. Recorded message again.*

DEREK (*off*). Food's nearly ready.

DAVID. Five minutes!

DEREK (*off*). I'm quite pleased with it if I say so myself!

ADVISER. Thanks for holding. How can I help you?

DAVID. I'm not a pervert.

ADVISER. Sir –

DAVID. Wait! I'm not drunk. I can't get my penis into the opening in the device.

ADVISER. Does it look broken at all?

DAVID. It curves upwards a bit.

ADVISER. Does the *Autosuck* look broken?

DAVID. I don't think so.

ADVISER. Have you tried it with lubricant?

DAVID. No, I –

ADVISER. People don't use it because they think they'll get electrocuted but it's very safe.

DAVID. It won't help.

DEREK *appears in the doorway with* DAVID*'s dinner on a plate. He stays there, quiet.*

ADVISER. Right...?

DAVID. I have cerebral palsy.

ADVISER. Oh. That's fine.

DAVID. I can't hold the device still to navigate my penis in.

ADVISER. Oh gosh, love! I don't think we've... What about elastic bands. Would they help?

DAVID. How?

ADVISER. I don't know.

DAVID. Do you have a funnel?

ADVISER. A funnel?

DAVID. To guide it in with.

ADVISER. I don't think so no, I haven't seen anything like that.

DAVID. I'll just return it then please.

ADVISER. I'm afraid if it's – Would a kitchen one work?

DAVID. No, I'll just return it.

ADVISER. I'm afraid if it's been used at all...

DAVID. I can't use it!

ADVISER. If you've had contact with it I'm afraid that would count as used.

DAVID. I can get my assistant to clean it.

DEREK *looks awkward.*

ADVISER. I'm sorry, love, if it's out of the box and it's not the device that's faulty...

DAVID. Great. A hundred and thirty pounds and I haven't even fucking spunked!

ADVISER. Please don't talk to me like that, sir.

DAVID. You work in a sex shop!

A moment.

ADVISER (much more coldly). I'm sorry. There's nothing I can do. (beat) You'll just have to use your hand.

DAVID. Can you listen! I can't. Are you fucking thick? I can't wank. I can't wank myself. I can't masturbate. Ever!

DAVID*'s arm swipes at the Autosuck, which flies across the room. It nearly hits* DEREK, *who drops the plate of food on the floor. They look at each other awkwardly. After a moment:*

ADVISER. Sir? Are you alright?

DAVID. Piss off.

He ends the call with a stab of his thumb. DEREK *looks at the food on the floor.*

DEREK. I'll get you some more. Let me clean this up first.

DEREK *vanishes to the kitchen and returns with kitchen paper and begins wiping the food up as he wonders what to say.*

There's probably something more specialist out there.

DAVID. I don't know.

DEREK. Can have a look.

DAVID *doesn't want to talk about it.*

Jill: Nearly home xx.

DAVID *physically reacts to this.*

You alright, buddy?

DAVID. Yeah.

DEREK. So um. I've got an audition.

DAVID. Congratulations.

DEREK. Yeah, thanks, buddy. So um. Do you think I could come a bit late in the morning?

DAVID. It's quite short notice.

DEREK. Yeah I only just got the email five minutes ago… You remember that production of *Private Lives* we saw that was set in Ibiza? It's the same girl directing.

DAVID. You said it was gimmicky.

DEREK. That was probably a bit harsh.

DAVID. The main guy was so hot.

DEREK. Well he was too young for it. And he was very… 'surface'. Anyway, everyone else seemed to like it. And they've got funding this time so there's decent pay. And actually it's a much better play than you'd think. A fucking good play, structurally. She wants to set it in Iraq – in Mosul? Where ISIS was.

DAVID. Yeah. What play is it?

DEREK *swaps the kitchen paper for a sponge and some cleaning spray.*

DEREK. So it's called *Run for Your Wife*. Do you know it?

DAVID. No.

DEREK. It's sort of a farce, essentially. There's a taxi driver who has two wives in two different houses and they don't know about each other, and he manages to live like that for years until one day his schedule goes tits-up because he intervenes in a fight and ends up getting injured. Except in this one what's going to kick it all off is a car bomb going off.

DAVID. Are you going to be the taxi driver?

DEREK. No! I'm not going for an Iraqi. That would be crass. No, it's for the neighbour – we're imagining him as a sort of NGO worker. Well not 'we', I haven't got it yet.

Pause while DAVID *enjoys the awfulness of this.*

DAVID. I really want you to get this part.

DEREK. Thanks, buddy.

DAVID. I'm going to be there every night. Will Adam be in it?

DEREK. Who's Adam?

DAVID. The hot guy in *Private Lives*.

DEREK. Oh.

DAVID. I talked to him in the bar. He was lovely.

DEREK. No he won't be in it.

DAVID. He was brilliant.

DEREK. He's going into *Hollyoaks*. Listen, buddy, if you still want me to help type your job applications it might need to wait till tomorrow.

DAVID. I forgot. The deadline's tomorrow. It doesn't matter.

We hear a key in the front door. In response.

DAVID. Don't tell Jill I haven't done them.

DEREK. Why?

DAVID. I stood her up to get them finished.

DEREK. I don't like lying. I'm not good at it. Not to Jill.

JILL enters, carrying a glass terrarium planted with a few succulents.

JILL. Hello, workers. Sorry, Derek, the film went on for days.

JILL holds the terrarium aloft.

David, this is for you.

DEREK. I think the budgie's escaped!

JILL. Very funny. Planted it myself, I hope it's alright.

DAVID. It's lovely! Thank you. You'll have to help me look after it.

JILL. It looks after itself, babe. (*She puts it down somewhere*.) There. Well we can decide where you want it. Anyway, see it as a little present for being disciplined and knuckling down. Even if you did cancel on me.

DEREK. How was the film?

JILL. I don't think I was in the right frame of mind for it. I'd gone straight from work. I tell you what, that place is knackering me. 'Come and run a terrarium shop with me,' she said. 'It'll be a laugh,' she said. I think it's having to interact with people. How did you get on?

DEREK (*extracting himself*). I'll get you some more dinner. Had a bit of an accident, didn't we?

JILL. No, love, you've been taking dictation all afternoon, I'll get it.

DEREK (*to* DAVID)....Is that okay?

DAVID. Yeah.

JILL. So. Do you want me to proofread anything?

DAVID. No.

JILL. You want to get it right.

DEREK. I'll just –

He disappears into the kitchen.

DAVID. I haven't quite finished.

JILL. Well give me five minutes I'll help you.

DAVID. No.

JILL. Oh. Please yourself.

She sees the Autosuck on the floor. She picks it up.

What's this?

She gets no answer. She turns it this way and that. Then she spots the open box that it came in, adorned with a photo of a man's face in mid-orgasmic ecstasy.

DAVID. It came today.

JILL (*laughing*). Oh my god! Well you'll have a nice evening to reward yourself. (*She puts two and two together.*) Is that why you cancelled on me? Have you been sat here using a wank machine? (*Beat.*) Derek, has he – ?

DEREK (*off*). No. Don't worry. Not here. In his room.

JILL. I don't care if it was in the front fucking garden.

She flings the toy away from her with a grimace.

DAVID. Derek!

DEREK. Sorry. I said I'm no good at lying.

JILL. David! I only chose that cinema because it's got the wheelchair space that you like.

She goes into the kitchen and talks from there.

Derek, move, I'm washing my hands.

We hear the tap running as she washes her hands.

It's three quid more than the Odeon and the carpets are disgusting. You told me you couldn't come because you had to submit the application by six o'clock.

DAVID. I got it wrong. It's tomorrow.

JILL returns.

I was excited.

JILL. Oh well that's very nice, isn't it.

DEREK returns with a plate of food and crouches next to DAVID to feed him.

DAVID. It's not just a wank to me.

DEREK gives DAVID a mouthful of food.

JILL. Oh it's an affair, is it? You and the wanking machine? Are you going to go off into the sunset together like those fucking robots in *Star Wars*?

DEREK. Droids.

DEREK gives DAVID a mouthful of food.

JILL. Can you stop eating when I'm trying to have a conversation?! It's rude.

She's addressed this to DAVID, but it's DEREK who looks like he's been slapped.

I'll do it in a minute. (*She calms.*) It's fine, Derek. Sorry. I'll do it.

DEREK. You sure?

DAVID nods. DEREK pops the plate down carefully on the desk and grabs his jacket.

He was only going to try it for a few minutes. But he couldn't get it to work. (*Pause. To DAVID.*) So is it okay if I come in after the audition tomorrow? I'll only be an hour or two.

DAVID. Jill, can you go to work late tomorrow?

JILL. No, I'm opening up.

DAVID. Sorry. Get them to rearrange it.

DEREK. Yeah, yeah. I'll see what they can do… You could see if one of the other assistants is free? Or I can, I'll see who's about. Or yeah, I'm sure they'll have another slot. Right.

Well, have a good night.

DEREK goes.

JILL. I could have done another shift.

DAVID. I wanted to have an orgasm.

JILL. Obviously.

DAVID. I wanted to know what it feels like.

JILL takes in the implication of this.

JILL. Oh babe. (*A moment, then, tenderly.*) Look… I've told you. You should get yourself on Grindr or something.

DAVID. Have you seen my fucking movements?

JILL. That's the beauty of going online, isn't it. Your movements won't be the first thing. You can chat first. Set out your stall. Be funny – you're funny. Be charming… you can manage that. First impressions.

DAVID. They'd see a picture of me.

JILL. You're cute.

DAVID. I look disabled.

JILL. Right. So that filters out all the dickheads who aren't interested. People want to have sex with all sorts of people.

DAVID. Even if I found someone desperate enough to meet me they'd run away as soon as they saw me twitching.

JILL. 'What do you want in a lover?' 'I just want someone who stays really still.'

DAVID. Have you ever seen anyone in porn that looks like me?

JILL. Porn isn't exactly famous for its diversity or realism.

DAVID. But it does have people who can walk and talk properly.

JILL (*thinks about this*). I don't see why it needs to.

DAVID. They don't just have sex. Sometimes at the start they play volleyball or they're in a swimming pool.

JILL. David, this is Britain, nobody is going to make you play volleyball before you have sex with them. Anyway I'm not interested in porn.

DAVID. You spend a lot of time in your room.

JILL. Not watching porn!

DAVID. You're like a nun. *You* don't get laid.

JILL *wants to deny this but can't.*

It's over a year since you broke up with Darren. You deserve someone nice.

JILL. So do you. And it's not me standing people up for an oversexed kitchen appliance.

Pause. JILL gets the plate of food and gives DAVID a mouthful.

And you can't keep putting off finding a job. You're bored.

DAVID. I've got a job.

JILL. Volunteering for a community newsletter.

DAVID. It's an online newspaper. (*Beat.*) It's difficult.

JILL. I was reading, apparently employment is actually going up.

DAVID. I can't do junior jobs. I can't pour a pint. I can't carry folders. I'm shit on the phone. Why can't I just be paid to write? I did an internship at *The Times* for God's sake.

JILL. I know. But everyone does work experience.

DAVID. Hardly anyone gets on that.

JILL. I know. But… maybe you got that because. You know.

She gives DAVID a mouthful. It takes a while to chew.

DAVID. We can see a film next week.

JILL. I'm not making any more plans with you until you get your arse online.

DAVID. You can't force me to have sex. That's rape.

JILL. David.

You're the one making assumptions about people. (*Beat.*) You know what guys are like, they'll go for anything.

DAVID *reacts to this.*

I mean… there's probably people who actively go for people like – people with impairments. I don't know. (*Beat.*) They might be into… I dunno.

DAVID. Dribbling.

JILL. Dribbling! I've heard weirder – oh my god did you know you can get these kinky chairs with a sort of toilet seat in them and someone puts their face under it and, well...

DAVID. I'm not going on Grindr.

JILL. Well what then?

DAVID. One day the right guy will come along.

JILL. When? You're twenty-five. (*Beat.*) It's not like you to be a coward. (*Beat.*) Don't stand me up again.

Scene: David and Mani Return from a Triumph

A PowerPoint slide showing a photo of DAVID *and the text:*

> Thank you for listening. David Hunter.
> Twitter: @DavidHunter5

The sound of applause, which fades as we go into...

Late evening/night. 11.30, 12-ish. There are some bags of compost stacked up on the floor which get in the way of DAVID*'s chair when he comes into the lounge with his friend* MANI *– twenties, British Asian, bright colours.* DAVID *has a four-pack of beers on his lap.* MANI *helps* DAVID *take his coat off over the opening of their conversation.*

MANI. Warm in here.

DAVID. Yeah. I like it.

MANI. Alright, Nan, I'll get you your Ovaltine. You were amazing tonight.

DAVID. I'm actually really buzzing.

MANI. Seriously, you just like gave a talk to hundreds of people.

DAVID. Eighty-five.

MANI. Again?

DAVID. Eight-y-five.

MANI. No.

DAVID. I asked the woman.

MANI. Magda?

DAVID. With the beads.

MANI. She's a fucking downer. If you bought her flowers she'd say 'they'll be dead in a week'. Still. Eighty-five people who now know about the social model of disability. You had them eating out of your arse.

DAVID. Was the toilet story too much?

MANI. You know it wasn't.

DAVID. She didn't want to give me a glass of wine.

MANI. Magda? That's cos I told her you're a violent alcoholic.

DAVID. I just get angry sometimes.

MANI. What? I'm joking... Seriously, babe, I'm joking.

   MANI *takes the beers, opens two and leaves the room. He comes back.*

   Have you got a straw?

DAVID. Yeah. Coat pocket.

MANI. Again?

DAVID. Coat. Pocket.

   MANI *gets a silicone straw from* DAVID*'s coat.*

   My voice gets worse when I'm tired.

MANI. Say again?

DAVID. My, voice –

MANI. I'm kidding. I know it does. Nice that the boys came along. It was like you'd got groupies.

DAVID. I told them there'd be a free bar.

MANI. Shane was quite restrained considering. I thought he was gonna heckle.

DAVID. I would have loved that.

MANI. Or try and fuck a fresher.

MANI puts the straw in one of the cans and holds it up to DAVID's mouth for him to have a good drink from. DAVID nods when he's had enough.

You know I was joking about the… violent thing.

DAVID. Yeah.

MANI. No it's nice not to be out on a Saturday.

DAVID. We've been out.

MANI. Yeah but *out*-out.

DAVID. You can go and join them. I don't mind.

MANI. No! No. I'm serious. This is great. Nice change. Can't be healthy, can it, every week. Chemicals, out all night…

DAVID. Sex.

MANI. It'll be nice to wake up on a Sunday morning for once.

DAVID. Especially now that you're a vicar.

MANI. A vicar?! Fuck, can you imagine.

DAVID. You'd be good. (*Beat.*) You were very impressive tonight.

MANI. Oh. Well.

DAVID. Is that your job then?

MANI. What do you mean?

DAVID. Performing like that.

MANI. Performing! I was just talking.

DAVID. It was like performing.

MANI. No. You know what my job is. I give advice to students who've plagiarised essays or got their knob out in the canteen or otherwise bollocksed things up. Fuck knows why anyone trusted me with that. This was just a thing. I host them sometimes.

DAVID. Everyone was laughing.

MANI. Were they?

DAVID. And not just at what you're wearing.

MANI. Haha fuck off. Anyway what about you, eh. They were lapping it up.

DAVID. You should be a professional comedian.

MANI. Anyway, cheers. (*Lifts his can.*)

DAVID. You used to do comedy gigs at university.

MANI (*deflecting*). Shall we put some music on?

DAVID. Yeah. I really liked Simon.

MANI. Oh my god. Everyone likes Simon. He's straight. Well. He let me suck him off in the union toilets last year when he was high, but I think he was being kind mainly.

DAVID. He's so handsome and kind.

MANI. Yeah alright.

DAVID. He got me more wine.

MANI. Trying to get you drunk, eh.

DAVID. He asked me about my Master's. He's lovely. (*Checks his phone, which rests on the seat of his chair between his legs.*) He hasn't accepted my friend request yet.

MANI. He doesn't really do Facebook.

DAVID. I hate people who don't do Facebook.

MANI. Oh you hate him now, do you, that was a roller coaster.

DAVID. No I actually love him. Is he going to the club.

MANI. No I told you he's straight.

MANI holds the beer up for DAVID *to drink from. He drinks for a bit.*

It always feels like the straw's hitting the back of your throat or something. It's not, is it?

DAVID (*shakes his head. Then a new thought*). Does it make you horny?

MANI. What?? Horny?

DAVID. No, when you take drugs.

MANI. Oh… it can do.

DAVID. Apparently one of my meds is a bit like MDMA.

MANI. You know you could have come tonight if we'd gone on with them?

DAVID. You can still go.

MANI. Well it's not even that late yet.

DAVID. I don't mind.

MANI. No – no. Don't be daft. Music. (*He gets his phone out.*) Can I put it on your speaker?

DAVID. Yeah.

Dance music starts playing on a Bluetooth speaker.

Bit louder.

MANI. Is that alright with the neighbours?

DAVID. Fuck them. Their children wake me up.

MANI. Is Jill in?

DAVID. Probably.

MANI. I'll do it a *tiny* bit louder. There, see. Party at David's. Who needs to go out?!

Both their phones ping.

Was that you.

DAVID. I think it was both of us.

They look at their phones.

Shane: Come here!

A *photo of three young men in a club, one has his arm round another.*

Who is the boy with his arm round Russell? Is that the one he wanted to meet?

MANI. No I think he's the wrong colour. Dunno. Quick work.

DAVID. He's beautiful.

JILL *enters, in pyjamas and holding a Kindle.*

JILL. David, that wanker upstairs'll be banging on the floor.

DAVID. He's alright.

JILL. Well I'm kind of trying to sleep. I'm at the shop tomorrow. Sunday's our big day and we're doing a workshop-class thing. For fucking kids.

MANI. Hi Jill.

JILL. Hi Mani. Surprised you're not out painting the town pink.

MANI. No, I was toying with it but no, nice to have a quiet one.

JILL. Not *that* quiet.

MANI. Sorry. That's me. (*He turns the music down.*) I mean I could still go later. For a bit… No, that's stupid. I'll hang here. Then get an early one.

JILL. Not *that* early.

MANI. I could go for a run!

JILL. Is he mashed?

MANI. In the morning. Not been for a run in ages. Might go down the reservoir.

DAVID. Cruising?

MANI. What? No! I don't just have sex you know. (*Beat. Then, re: David.*) He was dead good tonight.

JILL. Oh! How'd it go? He spent ages writing that.

DAVID. Shane and Russell came.

JILL. Oh. And they went on without you?

DAVID. Russell wanted to meet up with some boy. Doesn't matter.

JILL. Well nice one, babe, I'm proud of you. Alright well, keep it down.

DAVID. Yes, Mum.

> JILL *goes*.

MANI. I'm not being funny right but if she was trying to sleep why was she holding her Kindle?

DAVID. She falls asleep with it on her face. I think you should go out.

MANI. What? No. (*He toys with the idea*.) Have some more beer and let's watch some shit on YouTube.

DAVID. I'm actually quite tired.

MANI. Well… no. Come on.

> *Their phones ping. They both look at them. It's obviously another message from their friends.*

DAVID. Go on. Join them.

MANI. Come with me.

DAVID. I can only access the ground floor in that place and that has the shit music.

> *A moment.*

> Go on. Suck a cock for me.

MANI. Are you sure?

DAVID. Yes.

MANI. Will you be alright?

DAVID. Yes.

A moment. MANI *lingers.*

You've never asked me if I've ever had sex.

MANI (*this has come out of nowhere*). Oh. Um. Well you've never asked *me*.

DAVID. You don't catch gonorrhoea just from going on the Victoria Line.

MANI. Three times last year, fucking hell. One day it'll be that drug-resistant strain and that'll be me for life. Oozing. We all will. The gays and drug-resistant gono will end up as one sort of symbiotic joint life form. Pus trails everywhere. See? There's benefits to not being a slut. (Pause. Slightly awkward.) I have wondered. Dunno, it just felt kind of a mean thing to ask? Not mean but – like asking a woman why she hasn't had children, or… (Beat.) Have you ever had sex?

DAVID. Do you think I've ever had sex?

MANI. Oh man, don't do that! 'How old do you *think* I am?' I always add a few years if anyone asks that. You have to add just enough that it's plausible you really think it. It's always guys I pull… (*Pause.*) I don't know if you've had sex. I guess I think you probably haven't.

DAVID. Yeah.

MANI. And that's like sex as in not just… Like a blowjob's sex, right? I count that as sex.

DAVID. Yeah.

MANI. Okay. I'm sorry. We should do something about that. (*Panics.*) I mean, not – But, is it something you want to fix?

DAVID. I'm actually really tired.

MANI. Have you met José? You should talk to José. Doesn't need to be him. He'll know others.

DAVID. I don't want to pay to have sex with someone because they've got a normal body.

MANI. No. (*Beat.*) Though fucking hell he hasn't really got a normal body, has he. It's amazing. (*Pause.*) Okay. Well, thank you. For tonight.

DAVID. Jill thinks I should go on fucking Grindr.

MANI weighs this up.

MANI. Maybe you should. (*Pause.*) Could just download it?

He reaches for DAVID's *phone.*

DAVID. I don't know.

MANI *finds the app to download.*

MANI. You can delete it any time. As I tell myself every three weeks. (*He hands the phone back.*) Any cunts, just block them, yeah? (*Beat.*) You were ace tonight. Do you need – Are you alright getting to bed?

DAVID. I'm fine.

MANI. Need the toilet?

DAVID. No I'm fine. Thank you for inviting me. Have fun.

MANI gives DAVID *a hug.*

MANI. Love you.

He goes. We hear the outside door open and close. Shortly afterwards, the music from the Bluetooth speaker sputters out as MANI's *phone goes out of range.* DAVID *sits there a while. Suddenly he flings his phone onto the floor. He shouts.*

DAVID. Jill! (*Beat.*) JILL! JILL JILL JILL JILL! (*Beat.*) JILL.

JILL *emerges.*

JILL. Babe, what's wrong?!

DAVID. I need to go to the toilet and I want to go to bed.

JILL. Jesus, I thought you were on fire. Mani's gone, has he?

DAVID. Yeah.

JILL. He could have helped you.

DAVID. It's not his job.

JILL. It's not about whose job it is.

DAVID. You live here for free. You assist me at night. It's not difficult.

JILL. Yes, alright.

DAVID. That's the deal! It's very clear. My phone.

JILL. What?

DAVID. My. Phone. Is. On. The. Fucking. Floor.

A moment. JILL *caves and picks it up.*

JILL. I'll put it on your bed.

DAVID. Why have we got compost in my living room?

JILL. I bollocksed up the delivery address.

DAVID. Are you trying to stop me escaping from a fire?

JILL. Yes.

DAVID. It's a fucking fire hazard. You'd get done for manslaughter.

JILL. I'll get done for murder if you carry on like this.

A moment as DAVID *lets that register.*

Come on.

Dating App Chat: XXL

XXL*'s pic is a fairly muscular chest.*

David: Hi

XXL: Hi.

David: How are you?

XXL: Horny.

David: Cool.

Pause.

David: What are you up to?

Pause.

David: Hi

XXL: U accom?

David: What?

XXL: Can I come to you.

Pause.

David: Yes please.

XXL: Location?

David: I should probably tell you I have
cerebral palsy.

XXL: I don't care about that.
How big?

David: Five foot five but I use a wheelchair

XXL: HOW BIG IS YOUR DICK

David: I haven't measured it.

Pause.

David: I can't hold a ruler.

Pause.

David: It's bigger than most.

XXL: Pic

David: I haven't got one. Have you?

XXL *sends a photo of an enormous erect*
cock. Suddenly the chat vanishes to a
point. XXL *has blocked him.*

Dating App Chat: Callum

CALLUM *is twenties, sharp haircut, trim/slim body. Could be in porn*.

> Callum: Looking to meet?

David: With you?

> Callum: No with Florence Pugh 😜
> Yes 😊

Callum sends a couple more pics: nude but not full-frontal. Nicely lit.

David: Wow.
I ha
I have cerebral palsy.

> Callum: I know what
> I'm doing 👍
> I've had disabled clients.

David: What kind of clients?

> Callum: I'm an escort. 💦📱

A moment.

David: I'm ok thanks
Sorry.

> Callum: Baby I'm sure you are nice.
> But someone like you will always
> have to pay for sex.

Scene: David's First Hook-Up

Day. DAVID *is in bed with* ROB, *a middle-aged man. They have had some kind of sex and are chilling. Onscreen the name 'Rob' appears briefly.*

ROB. *I* used to work in journalism. Photos for the local paper. Funny world. You'd get a call, jump in the car. Primary-school fancy-dress days. Someone off the telly doing a musical at the Grand. Couples looking sad and serious in front of the remains of their car... Giving things significance, really. This was back home, long time ago. I mainly do weddings now. (*Beat.*) I'd love to photograph you sometime.

DAVID. Are you joking?

ROB. I'd shoot you in bed. Not too revealing but in bed. The covers just up to here. Sunlight on the wall, just missing you. Eyes straight down the lens. (*Beat.*) You have a beautiful stomach.

DAVID (*with wonder*). My whole body feels calm! My voice feels clearer.

ROB. Does that usually happen?

DAVID....I don't actually know.

ROB *realises this is an important moment for* DAVID. *He doesn't say anything but gives him a kind smile and takes his hand.*

This isn't really what I expected.

ROB. What did you expect?

DAVID (*laughs*). I can't remember.

ROB. You sounded like you were having a whale of a time. It's nice.

They snuggle a bit. ROB *finds that* DAVID *is hard again.*

Someone's woken up again. Your dick is fantastic.

ROB *goes under the covers, and starts sucking* DAVID *off.*
After a while, ROB*'s phone rings. Without stopping, his arm*
goes searching for it and finds it. He emerges and looks at
the phone.

Do you mind?

DAVID. No.

ROB *answers the phone.*

ROB (*amiable, familiar*). Hello, love – Yeah, I saw your text,
are you there now? – Yeah, great, could you get kidney beans
for the chilli? I forgot – Thanks – Yeah hold on, I started a
list.

He holds his phone in front of him to glance at a note he's
written on it.

Salad cream, kitchen foil, tinned tomatoes… have we? Get
some anyway. Think that's it. Oh, see if they've got one of
those frozen strudels? Thanks, angel – Yeah see you soon.

He hangs up. A moment.

DAVID. Is that your boyfriend?

ROB. Husband. (*Pause.*) Don't worry, I'm allowed.

ROB *starts jerking* DAVID *off, and jerking himself off too.*
DAVID *is in ecstasy. After half a minute,* ROB *stops, reaches*
for his phone again and makes a call.

Sorry. (*Into his phone.*) Yeah, sorry, meant to say. Deodorant.
– Yeah, roll-on. Any brand. Thanks. (*He hangs up.*) I'd forget
my own head!

Text conversation: Rob Photo

6.48 p.m.

David: Really nice to you meet you x

                Rob Photo: You too x

David: When do you want to meet again?

David: ?

Scene: David and Jill Have News

Early evening. DAVID *and* DEREK. DEREK *is a little terse.*

DEREK. Well I'm glad one of us has some good news.

DAVID. He actually thought I was sexy. And he wasn't a weirdo at all.

DEREK. Well it's nice that you're setting the bar high. Are you going to see him again?

DAVID. Yeah. I really want to.

    DAVID *sends a text to 'Rob Photo':*

        David: Hi

    It felt amazing. My body feels so relaxed.

    We hear the front door opening and closing.

DEREK. I think your speech is a bit clearer.

DAVID. Yeah.

    JILL *enters with her coat on.*

JILL. David, you are not going to believe what's happened to me today, you are going to be so proud of me!

DAVID. What happened?

DEREK. Sounds like you've both got news.

JILL. Hello, Derek. (*To* DAVID.) What news?

> DAVID *is very happy and pleased with himself. He grins at her.*

> You look like you won the fucking EuroMillions. I'll put the kettle on.

> *She goes towards the kitchen.*

DEREK. I'll do that.

JILL. I can fill a kettle, Derek.

DEREK. It's fine, let me.

JILL. You don't drink tea.

DEREK. I drink herbal.

JILL. I think we ran out.

DEREK. Oh I know, I don't want one. I'm just saying.

JILL. Only twenty bags in a box I mean why even bother.

DEREK. Do you want one, David?

DAVID. No.

DEREK. Just you then.

JILL. Derek, I can make a cup of tea.

DEREK. It's alright, I'm still working. (*To* DAVID.) Oh, if that's alright?

DAVID (*exasperated, if amused*). I don't fucking care. Yes.

> DEREK *goes into the kitchen and puts the kettle on. He can come in and out of the kitchen while making* JILL *her tea.*

JILL. David, come on, tell me your news so I can tell you mine.

DAVID. You go first.

JILL. No! Yeah okay. Honestly you're not gonna believe this. Cos you know, the people we usually get coming in that shop - we get couples, we get women, and we get gay men, that's

pretty much it. But. So. This fella comes in the shop today.
I say fella, oh my god David he was practically a boy but
really very charming. He chooses the biggest terrarium case
we had and asks me to help him pick all the bits for planting
it. We had a right natter. And you know sometimes they're
a bit exhausting, the talkers, because you're sort of trapped
in the conversation with them until they buy something or
leave but I could have gone on all afternoon. He likes art, he
does meditation – I could tell you his life story. I think he's
quite new to London. Anyway so, when he's paid up and said
goodbye about twenty times – I'm not even exaggerating –
I'm sat there thinking, 'That was nice, Jill, nice young man,
little flirt, bit of progress,' just then I notice it right there in
front of me, on the counter. He must have done it while I was
bagging up for him. I didn't think that sort of thing happened
these days. I thought it was all, you know, swipes and likes
or the occasional bit of mild sexual assault in a bar. Just goes
to show.

DAVID. I actually don't know what you're talking about.

JILL. His phone number! He left his phone number. He's
fucking gorgeous, David, even his handwriting was fit. I'm
going to have to get down the pool. Lose some of this gut.

DEREK. What gut?!

JILL. The one on my elbow Derek, which gut do you think?
(To DAVID.) He must be earning a fair bit – not that I give
a toss – but he spent best part of hundred and fifty quid on a
tank of tiny fucking plants and that's not inconsiderable at his
age.

DAVID. How old is he?

JILL. Don't ask. Can't be more than twenty-four.

DEREK. I wish I'd met someone like you when I was twenty-
four. Nice older woman.

JILL *gives* DEREK *the briefest of stares at this.*

JILL. Anyway we're seeing an exhibition on Sunday. I'm a bit wary of an exhibition as a first date because you don't want to be standing there looking at a picture and completely failing to getting anything from it while they're looking at it like it's the *Mona Lisa* in 3D but I'll go with the flow. So! You had some news.

DAVID. It doesn't matter.

DEREK. Cupid's been a busy boy today.

DAVID. Leave it.

JILL. Don't do that.

DAVID. It's nothing. It's my business.

JILL. David! Spill. What's this about Cupid?

DAVID. I met a man. It doesn't matter.

JILL. Oh my god! Met as in…?

DAVID. Yeah

JILL. You horny goat! What's he like?

DAVID. It was just sex.

JILL. You say that now! (*Beat.*) How old is he?

DAVID. Fifty.

Pause.

DEREK. Sugar daddy.

JILL. I didn't know you went for older guys. Well I hope he was nice.

DAVID. He's lovely.

JILL. Well good on you. Good on us. This is where they both turn out to be psychos. Or married.

A moment.

DAVID. He's married.

JILL. Oh.

DAVID. To a man.

JILL. David!

DAVID. They have an open relationship.

JILL. Is that what he told you?

DAVID. Lots of people have them.

JILL. Jesus, you're greedy you lot, aren't you.

DAVID. It was only sex.

JILL.…Yeah. Good on you! Well, now you've got over that
     hurdle the world is your oyster. Look out, London.

DEREK. Shall I be off?

DAVID. Yeah.

JILL. Yeah night, Derek.

DEREK. I um. I didn't get the gig. The play – I didn't get it.

JILL. Oh darling.

DAVID. You said you hadn't heard.

DEREK. No, well, I had heard.

DAVID. Are you okay?

DEREK. Yeah, yeah. Actor's life.

DAVID. Do you want a beer?

DEREK. No, no. (*Beat.*) They had to rearrange my audition
     slot to really early in the morning, before they were meant
     to start. It's all they had. I wasn't really with it, I don't think
     they were either really. Faffing with coffees. So. (*Beat.*)
     Right.

He goes. A little later we hear the front door.

JILL. Don't get involved, David.

DAVID. It's only sex.

JILL. He's married.

DAVID. Of course he's married, he's lovely! (*Beat*.) I came so hard I hit my own face.

JILL *stares at him*.

JILL. I'll have to buy a hat.

Text Conversation: Rob Photo

10.05 p.m.

David: Hi. We should do it again.

                    Rob Photo: Sure! Take it easy.

David: When? Xx

11.32 p.m.

David: Hi.
How are you.

8.32 a.m.

David: ?

4.10pm

David: Hi.

The screen sputters, transitions to:

Dating App Conversation: Mark, various app users

MARK *is wearing a hoodie and sunglasses*.

                    Mark: More pics?

David: On my Instagram

Mark: Nudes?

David: No

Mark: Take some

David: I can't

Mark: Bullshitter

David: I physically can't hold my phone.

Mark: Bye

Then a barrage of messages from various chats (but these could work as a chaotic soundscape of demanding voices):

Student: More pics?

TwinkTop: Show me more

Ben: Lemme see it

2forMore: Show me ur cock

Slut: Body pics?

James: Bod pics?

Stockwell: Bod?

Now: Butt?

Ryan: Can I see your dick

BritneyBitch: Can I see your arse

SE1: Show me your hard cock

Oscar: Show me what your gonna put in me

GroupFun: Lemme see your hole

Coffee: Dick

Simon: Cock

Skyrim: More?

MANI (*a voicenote*). Hey babe, just saw your message. So the gays wanna see the size of your dowry do they?! Yeah, I suppose that's tricky innit, I hadn't thought about that. Guess you can't really ask a paid assistant to take a photo of your hard on can you! …Can you? Well, maybe I um… I… I'm sure you'll think of something! You always do!

Scene: A Hook-Up

On screen, the name 'RAY' appears briefly.

DAVID *is with* RAY, *an older man.* DAVID *is in his chair.*

RAY. You're a sexy little boy, aren't you.

DAVID. I don't know.

RAY. Aren't you, eh? A sexy little boy.

Without warning RAY *scoops* DAVID *out of the chair and onto the sofa. Opens his jeans.*

A naughty sexy little boy with a sexy big willy. And a sexy tight little bumbum.

RAY *starts wanking* DAVID *off. After a bit:*

DAVID. Can you take a picture of my dick?

RAY. You what?

DAVID. Can you take. A photo. Of my dick.

RAY. A photo of your big dickywick.

DAVID. Yeah.

RAY. Your big sucky lollicock.

DAVID. Yeah.

RAY *reaches for his own phone.*

On *my* phone.

RAY *doesn't understand or ignores this.*

No. *My* phone. *My* phone.

RAY *gets* DAVID*'s phone.*

Make it look good.

RAY *takes some photos.*

RAY. Naughty little boy! Shall I text that to your daddy?

DAVID. No!

RAY *plays with* DAVID*'s phone.*

RAY. Shall I find daddy's number?

DAVID. No!!

RAY *puts the phone down. He starts jerking* DAVID *off again.*

RAY. Are you a naughty boy? Are you a naughty boy with his naughty pictures? That's better. Good boy. Be good for daddy. That's it. That's it. Yes. Yes.

DAVID *orgasms.*

You come like a twelve-year-old!

Scene: David Meets Michael

JILL *and* DAVID *in the lounge. They've been watching something on TV –* JILL *is holding the remote.*

JILL. So?

DAVID. What?

JILL. 'What'?! What do you think? He's nice, isn't he?

DAVID. Yeah.

JILL. I know he's young but there's an old head on him.

DAVID. He's not that young.

JILL. Oh listen, don't forget I'm away weekend after next.

DAVID. Yeah. I'll find someone to stay over.

MICHAEL *enters. He's an amiable and attractive young man, a bit too keen to be friendly.*

MICHAEL. That toilet's a sweet bit of kit, isn't it. Does everything, does it?

DAVID. Yeah.

MICHAEL *sits next to* JILL *and puts an arm round her, very snuggly.*

MICHAEL. Looks like it'd even read to you while you do your business. How much do you pay for something like that?

DAVID. Three thousand two hundred pounds.

MICHAEL. Three…

DAVID. Three thousand two hundred pounds.

MICHAEL. Shit. You can go to Thailand for less. (*To* JILL, *an idea*.) Shall we go on holiday, babe?

JILL (*absolutely stunned*). A holiday?

MICHAEL. Why not?

JILL. Well. No I'd love to I just. It's so soon. (*Beat*.) I mean it would kind of have to be something cheap.

MICHAEL. Cheap I can do. Hostels all the way, isn't it. More authentic anyway. I stayed in this one in Marrakesh, in a riad, yeah? It was fucking sweet, rooftop bar, playing cards. Bit of a cheeky smoke.

DAVID. Why was it cheeky?

MICHAEL. Say again, dude?

DAVID. Why was it cheeky?

MICHAEL. Well… marijuana, it's like illegal? I think.

DAVID. Did you do a cheeky murder too?

JILL. Ignore him.

MICHAEL. It's his flat, babe! (*To* DAVID.) Not going to ignore you, am I.

MICHAEL *gets his phone out and scrolls through some photos till he finds one. He shows it to* JILL *and then* DAVID.

This was the riad, view from the top. (*He swipes to another.*) This is the beach at Essaouira. Massive for surfing. I've still got those Speedos somewhere.

DAVID *can't help gasping 'fuck' at the picture of him in Speedos.*

So Jill tells me you're a bit of a player, eh?

JILL. I didn't say that! I told him about your situation.

DAVID. I don't mind.

MICHAEL. No yeah fair play, man, that's tough. Sounds like you got it all sorted though. Get a man in every day.

DAVID. It's not every day.

JILL. No it's… every couple.

DAVID. It's twice a week.

JILL. Alright.

DAVID. It's not that much.

MICHAEL. I dunno, man, that sounds plenty. I'm not judging!

JILL. Yeah we're not judging.

DAVID. How often do you wank?

JILL. David!

DAVID. It's the same thing.

MICHAEL. Yeah it's a fair… Dunno. Depends. A couple…
Three… or four times a week.

JILL. Really?

MICHAEL. I think that's normal?

JILL. Wow.

MICHAEL. Babe. Don't you?

JILL. Not four times a week.

DAVID. Jill doesn't really like porn.

JILL. What? I didn't say that.

MICHAEL. I don't really. Well not the regular stuff.

JILL. This sounds interesting.

DAVID *laughs*.

MICHAEL. Oh! No! Nothing like that no just it always feels a
bit fake. I quite like those – Well, doesn't matter.

JILL. What?

MICHAEL. When it's real people live on camera.

JILL. You're chatting with women?

MICHAEL. No! Babe. No like live camera feeds. You just
watch.

DAVID. Cam Four.

MICHAEL. Yeah that's it! You look at that, do you?

DAVID. Not really. It's quite frustrating.

MICHAEL. Oh yeah I see. Cos you can't… (*Beat*.) I just like
seeing real couples. They look like they actually like each
other, you know? Not just… 'yeah take it yeah take it'.
(*Beat*.) How did we get onto this?

JILL. Well you'll have to show me. Right, we've discussed
toilets and porn and Casanova here, shall we watch the film?
Oh, we bought popcorn, I'll make popcorn.

JILL *gets up and exits into the kitchen. We hear sounds of a packet being opened, the microwave door closing, the microwave starting up.*

MICHAEL. Can I ask you something? Tell me if it's inappropriate. When you're on the er... on Grindr or whatever, how hard do you find it? I mean how many people don't find it – I dunno this sounds offensive... but people who don't find it weird.

DAVID. I'm more articulate when I'm typing.

MICHAEL. Sure.

DAVID. And I have a big penis.

MICHAEL. Oh yeah?

DAVID. That helps.

MICHAEL. Yeah I'm sure it does help. (*Beat.*) I've had experiences, you know.

DAVID. With men?

JILL *comes back in from the kitchen.*

MICHAEL. Yeah.

JILL. What are you saying?

DAVID. Michael's had experiences with men.

MICHAEL. Yeah, you know, like...

JILL. Gay experiences?

MICHAEL. Two or three. In my time.

JILL. 'In your time'? You're twenty-three.

MICHAEL. I said I was bi.

JILL. Yeah, you did. I didn't really think about it.

MICHAEL. You alright?

JILL. Yeah! No, it's nice, really. They probably can't resist you.

DAVID. How old were you?

MICHAEL. The first one when I was twelve with a school mate.

JILL. Oh! Well.

MICHAEL. The last one was in November.

The microwave beeps. JILL *goes to get the popcorn.*

DAVID. I don't know what I'd do if I was straight. You can't really expect a woman to pop over for fifteen minutes and wank you off.

MICHAEL. Do you worry about getting addicted?

Pause while DAVID *thinks.*

DAVID. When I ejaculate it makes my muscles relax. For the next five hours I feel amazing.

MICHAEL. Right. Wow. (*Beat.*) So it's not just that you really like dick then! (*Beat.*) But you only just started doing stuff with guys, didn't you? So like you must have managed for… years.

DAVID. I didn't know. It's harder when you know.

JILL *comes back with a big bowl of popcorn, hand-feeds a piece or two to* DAVID, *then sits with* MICHAEL. *She offers him the bowl.*

MICHAEL. Ah, love you, babe.

JILL (*pleasantly startled*). Do you?

MICHAEL. Sorry that just came out. Sorry.

JILL. Don't say sorry.

MICHAEL. No I know. Just weird to… Like that.

JILL. It's nice. You can say it again properly later.

She gives him a quick kiss.

Right. Film.

DAVID. I want to go to bed.

JILL. Now? It's early.

DAVID. I know.

JILL. Oh come on. I just got settled.

DAVID. I want to go to bed.

Grindr Chat: L

David: Want to swap pics?

L: What kind of pics?

David: 😈

Scene: David Meets Liam

On screen, the name 'LIAM' appears briefly.

Night. Bedroom. DAVID *is in bed with* LIAM *(twenties). He has a sporty, built physique. They look very comfortable together.* LIAM*'s fingers absentmindedly stroke* DAVID*'s chest or shoulder or wherever his hand is lying.*

DAVID. Fuck.

LIAM. Yeah that was decent, wasn't it.

DAVID. It was the best sexual experience I've ever had.

LIAM *laughs, a little nervously.*

It was like when I fantasise about sex. I thought it would be old men wanking me off forever.

LIAM. Mate.

DAVID. It was really spontaneous.

LIAM. It's meant to be, isn't it. I hate all that 'what you into' crap. (*Beat.*) I'm glad it wasn't your first time.

DAVID. Why?

LIAM. I dunno. Just…

DAVID. You were brilliant.

LIAM. I'll take that.

The calm is interrupted by music – an aggressive dance track coming from a phone at full volume. DAVID *has a very strong physical bodily reaction to it.*

Mate – shit – what's wrong? Mate.

He reaches under DAVID*'s neck and retrieves his phone.*

It's just my alarm. You were lying on it.

He silences it. DAVID *calms down. Catches his breath.*

DAVID. Sorry. Sorry.

LIAM. Fucking hell. Are you alright?

DAVID. Shit. Sorry.

LIAM. Stop saying sorry, what's wrong?

DAVID. Nothing. A reaction.

LIAM. Well obviously. Sorry.

DAVID. It's okay. Fuck. Sorry.

LIAM. Shall we both stop saying sorry?

A moment. They lie together, calm.

DAVID. Why have you got an alarm set for eleven-thirty p.m.?

LIAM. I was having a nap and needed to be up for something.

DAVID. You weren't having a nap.

LIAM. No, few weeks ago. I keep forgetting to cancel it properly. I just turn it off when it goes off.

DAVID *laughs.*

What?…

DAVID. Why don't you cancel it now?

LIAM. Yeah. Nice one.

He does, then sits up.

I should get going.

DAVID *reacts physically to this news.*

What was that one for?

DAVID. Sorry. Nothing. Sorry. (*Beat.*) You can go if you want.

LIAM. Obviously, I know I can.

But he doesn't move.

DAVID. It was my first time being fucked.

LIAM. Are you normally a top then?

DAVID *laughs.* LIAM *tickles him.*

Are you a big butch top?

DAVID *laughs uncontrollably.* LIAM *stops tickling him.*

DAVID. I've never tried.

LIAM. You should. You'd do some fucking damage, mate.

DAVID. My first time with a guy was three months ago.

LIAM. Ever?

DAVID. Yeah.

LIAM. And you can't wank.

DAVID. Yeah.

LIAM. And you're twenty-five.

DAVID. Yeah.

LIAM. What did you before that?

DAVID. I had anger-management therapy.

LIAM *laughs. Then stops.*

LIAM. What, for real?

DAVID. Yeah.

LIAM *sits with that for a moment.*

LIAM. I should be charging you by the hour then.

DAVID. How did you feel when you saw the way I move?

LIAM. You're fucking direct aren't you? (*He thinks.*) It's your voice that's weirder to be honest.

DAVID *reacts to this.*

LIAM. Got over it, didn't I. (*Beat*) We've all got our things.

DAVID. You haven't.

LIAM. Are you kidding?

DAVID. What things?

LIAM. Fucking hell, you only just met me!

DAVID. You must have had lots of experience.

LIAM. Dunno. I'm not a slut or anything.

DAVID. It doesn't matter if you are.

LIAM. I get what I need. I don't do relationships.

DAVID *reacts physically to this.*

DAVID. People always say things like that and then you see them at Tate Modern with hashtag boyfriends and the next week they've got a dog.

LIAM. Just, you've known me an hour yeah? Can you not tell me what I mean.

A moment.

DAVID. Can you pass me my drink?

LIAM *looks about for it.* DAVID *points vaguely towards it as well as she can.*

LIAM (*kindly*). Oh my god never direct traffic, I can't see where you're –

DAVID. On the table.

LIAM *puts the drink in* DAVID*'s hand, expecting him to take it. It falls on the floor, spilling.*

My fault. I need you to hold it.

LIAM. I'm not a mind-reader.

LIAM *takes a towel from the floor and uses it to soak up the spill. When he's done he stands up.*

DAVID. You are so fucking hot.

LIAM (*not unkindly*). Shut up.

LIAM *starts looking about for his T-shirt.*

DAVID. You're like a god. (*Beat.*) You're like an Instagram celebrity from Brazil.

LIAM. Don't be weird.

DAVID. Or from LA. You're like a painting. You look like *David*.

LIAM. *David*?

DAVID. The statue.

LIAM *pulls on the T-shirt.* DAVID *reacts physically.*

LIAM. What now?

DAVID. Are you going?

LIAM. I'm getting you some more water. Sir.

DAVID. Why did you put your T-shirt on?

LIAM. Because it's mine.

DAVID. Ha ha.

LIAM. Is that sarcastic?

DAVID. Yes.

LIAM. It's hard to tell. (*Beat.*) I'm self-conscious. You made me self-conscious.

DAVID. What the fuck are you actually talking about?

LIAM (*pinching his stomach*). I look shit at the moment.

DAVID. You need glasses.

LIAM. Stop staring at me.

DAVID. What's going on? It's me that moves like an angry squid.

LIAM. I haven't worked out in fourteen weeks. I told you. My fucking injury. (*Points to his chest and shoulders*.) I used to be really big here. And I didn't have this fucking tummy. It's – it's really stressing me out. I don't want to talk about it.

DAVID. Can you still get me my water.

LIAM. Oh, yeah.

He exits with the glass. Sound of a tap from the bathroom. He comes back and holds it for DAVID *to take a sip of it.*

You know what's really insane? I actually can, now. I can start working out. I can go to the gym. I can do anything. Two weeks ago, told me it was okay. But I haven't been. I can't make myself go. I've got this mental block, this... wall. Stopping me going back. Like I'm scared to. Because of how far I've slipped. I nearly go. Even get my gear on. Then I don't. I tell myself I'll go later, or tomorrow. But then I just sit there on the sofa in my gym kit doing nothing because if I did something else instead I'd be admitting to myself that I'm not going to go. And so I feel worse. I don't know what's wrong with me. I'm stuck. I can't look at myself in the mirror without a top on. I have to be fully dressed to clean my teeth.

Long pause.

I should get going.

A slight physical reaction from DAVID.

DAVID. I didn't mean to upset you.

LIAM. No, I just should just get off that's all. (Not unkind.) You lie there like you're the only one with anything going on but you're happy. You seem happy. You seem normal.

DAVID. Are you depressed?

LIAM. No! Not everything needs a label.

DAVID. Who do you talk to?

LIAM. What do you mean?

DAVID. Who do you talk to when you're down?

LIAM. Fucking hell, you warned me about your movements, you didn't say you were going to interrogate me.

DAVID. What about your parents?

LIAM. I'm an adult.

DAVID. I talk to my parents all the time.

LIAM. That's different obviously.

DAVID. Why?

LIAM. I don't want to talk about my family.

DAVID. Why?

LIAM. I just don't. They're fucked up.

DAVID. How do they make you feel?

LIAM. What? I don't know. (Beat.) They make me feel angry.

DAVID. My mum's amazing.

LIAM. Mine's a mess.

DAVID. I tell her everything.

LIAM. You going to tell her you got bummed?

DAVID. Yeah.

LIAM. Don't!

DAVID. I won't call it that.

LIAM. Anal intercourse.

DAVID. Yeah.

LIAM. 'He inserted his glans into my anus.'

DAVID. He filled my rectum with his penis.

LIAM. Mate.

Pause.

DAVID. Stay a bit.

LIAM. …I'm a bit talked out.

DAVID. We don't have to talk. We've got the rest of our lives to talk.

LIAM *flinches at that.*

LIAM. I said I don't do relationships.

DAVID. Sorry. I know. Sorry. I'm just a bit high.

LIAM. Fuck, man. I thought you weren't one of those.

DAVID. Medical drugs. They help control my movements. But they make me feel high.

LIAM. So am I actually talking to you? Or some… Is this even you?

DAVID. Yes!

A moment.

Can I have some water?

LIAM *sits on the bed with* DAVID *and takes the water with him. He holds it to* DAVID's *mouth so he can drink it.*

LIAM. More?

DAVID. Yeah.

He drinks some more.

LIAM. Thirsty.

DAVID. I worked up a sweat.

LIAM *laughs.*

I'm sorry things aren't ideal for you.

LIAM (*laughing slightly*). I'm sorry things aren't ideal for you.

DAVID. It's just who I am. Wishing I could walk is like looking at a bird and wishing I could fly.

LIAM. Yeah well. I'm impressed by your attitude. (*Beat*.) I haven't been with anyone with disabilities.

DAVID. I don't have disabilities

LIAM (*thinks he's joking*). That's the spirit!

DAVID. I'm a disabled man. (*Off his confused look*.) It doesn't matter.

LIAM. No, tell me.

DAVID. I have impairments, but I'm disabled because water is kept in kitchen taps that I can't use or reach.

LIAM. You're a pedantic man.

DAVID. Language is how society thinks about stuff. And people should be able to choose how they're talked about.

LIAM. Yes! (Pause) Okay. You have… impairments.

DAVID. Yeah

LIAM. And a very tight arsehole.

A moment.

DAVID. I didn't think I would ever get to be with someone like you.

LIAM. Don't do that.

DAVID. Why?

LIAM. It's bullshit. You're nice-looking. And you're funny.

DAVID. Your legs are amazing. The muscles. It must feel amazing when you run.

A moment.

LIAM. Can I pick you up?

DAVID. Why.

LIAM. Can I?

DAVID. Yes.

> LIAM *picks* DAVID *up, holding him in an embrace, and runs about the room with him. He returns him to the bed. A pause.*

LIAM. Just thought you might want to run about.

DAVID. That was very sweet and very hot and very strange.

LIAM. What do you do, normally? If you need water and stuff?

DAVID. I have people to help me.

LIAM. What people?

DAVID. Assistants.

LIAM. Like nurses?

DAVID. Just normal people. I choose them. I get money from social services so I can pay them. It means I'm in control.

LIAM. So do they like shower you and stuff?

DAVID. No. I lick myself clean like a cat.

> LIAM *laughs.*

Yes they shower me.

LIAM. Does it get sexy?

DAVID. Not really.

LIAM. You never fancy your assistants?

DAVID. I fancy everyone.

LIAM. Classy, mate.

DAVID. But you're hotter than everyone. (*Beat.*) One of them used to strip down to his pants to shower me so he wouldn't get wet. I had to think about disgusting things. (*Beat.*) What do you do?

LIAM. Why does it matter?

DAVID. Nothing matters.

LIAM. My job doesn't say anything about me. It's not what I wanted to do.

DAVID. What did you want to do?

LIAM. Don't laugh.

DAVID. I might.

LIAM. A footballer.

DAVID. Are you joking?

LIAM. I wanted to be a professional player. I almost was.

DAVID. Was it your injury?

LIAM. No. Do we have to have this conversation?

DAVID. All I know is your age and height.

LIAM. Go on.

DAVID. You're twenty-three.

LIAM. Well done. Height?

DAVID. Whatever it said on your profile.

LIAM *laughs*.

And you prefer to be a top unless you're in the right mood. (*Beat.*) And you're about six inches.

LIAM. Seven. Closer to seven.

DAVID. Nobody's listening. (*Beat.*) Stay the night.

LIAM. Okay.

DAVID. Do you want to put the light out.

LIAM *does. They lie in the dark for a while. Then:*

LIAM. I'm a pretty good player. Naturally pretty good. I was the best at my school, but that doesn't really mean... And I really enjoyed playing. But there's something missing. In the end, there was something missing. I couldn't keep up with the training. I couldn't work hard enough. I got behind. I lost confidence. I suppose... I suppose I didn't want it enough.

I *wanted* to want it enough. But I think my brain just isn't built like that. And that's fucking devastating. (*Long pause*.) People talk about ambition. How you've got to have it. How some people don't have enough of it. But what can you do about that? It's like, *you* couldn't suddenly start being able to run just by trying harder. Your legs don't work like that. How are you meant to be more ambitious if that bit of your brain just isn't big enough? (*Beat*.) Can drive you mad thinking about it. (*Pause*.) Are you asleep?

DAVID. No. (*Pause*.) I'll tell my mum you're eight inches if you like.

Text Conversation: Liam

David: Have a brilliant morning.

Liam: You too man.

David: Thanks xxxxx

How was your day?

Liam: Yeah good you?

David: What did you do?

David: Hi.

David: How are you?

David: Hi Liam

David: How are you?

David: Hey.

David: Hi

Liam: Hi

David: How are you?

David: What are you up to?

David:?

David: Hi

David: ?

David: ?

David: ?

Scene: A Change of Plan

JILL *and* DAVID *are peering into* DAVID*'s terrarium.*

JILL. I can't see anything.

DAVID. There's definitely a bug in there.

JILL. Well it can't get out, it's a sealed environment. I thought you were going to put it in your bedroom? How's your article coming on?

DAVID. I can't concentrate, can I.

JILL. Babe, it was a shag. It's been two weeks. Move on.

DAVID. He picked me up! He picked me up and carried me and I felt safe and secure. It was like I'd never have to worry about anything ever again.

JILL. But that's not really about him, is it? It's about you.

DAVID *reacts, anxious or on the verge of tears.*

Hey. At least you'll get a change of scenery this weekend at your parents'. Here, you can help me.

JILL *exits and comes back with two dresses. A black one, and a colourful one with sequins or sparkles.*

For Saturday night. Which one do you think?

DAVID. Is it a fancy-dress party?

JILL. No?

DAVID. Is it a fancy-dress party with a circus theme?

JILL. No! You fucker.

DAVID (*laughing*). Wear the black one.

JILL. Really? (*Beat.*) Maybe you're right. I could zhuzh it up with something.

JILL *sits down, a bit deflated.* DAVID *gets a text from Liam:*

Liam: Hey.

DAVID *reacts strongly, physically.*

You alright?

David: WTF?

Liam: How's it going?
Had a good week?

A belt or something, do people do that?

David: Two weeks.

Liam: Been thinking about you.

David: I thought you weren't interested.

Liam: Do you want to meet up
this weekend?

A very strong reaction from DAVID.

What's wrong?

DAVID. Can you stay here this weekend?

JILL. This weekend? No, of course not.

DAVID. Just overnight.

JILL. It's a hen weekend! That's why you're going to your mum's.

DAVID. Please. Liam wants to meet.

JILL. Oh! Jesus, he blows hot and cold, doesn't he. See him in the week.

DAVID. He's taken two weeks to talk to me.

JILL. I'm sure he'll wait a couple of days more.

DAVID. What if he sees someone else instead?

JILL. Baby, you've met once. He can see who he likes.

DAVID. What if likes them more?

JILL. Well if he does like this entirely hypothetical person more, that's how dating works.

DAVID. It's different for me. (*Beat*.) He's like a fucking angel. (*Beat*.) There aren't many angels, you know. Can't you just go for the afternoon?

JILL. It's in Leeds! I'm not missing this so you can get laid. She was my third best friend at school and frankly I'm really touched to be asked.

DAVID. Is Michael going?

JILL. No it's a hen do. Just women. And one gay man. The 'life and soul' apparently so he's probably unbearable.

DAVID. Michael's a bit gay.

JILL. He was trying to bond with you, it was nice of him.

Liam: Don't worry about it.

DAVID *reacts quite frenziedly.*

David: Yes I want

What about Derek?

DAVID. All my regulars are busy. It's why I'm going home.

JILL. Have you asked Mani?

DAVID. I like to keep him as a friend.

JILL. He helps you all the time.

DAVID. If I happen to be seeing him. I'd rather keep that separate.

JILL. Right. I see. Well, up to you.

Text Conversation: Mani

David: Can you stay at mine this weekend?

Mani: I'm going to a
protest Saturday.

David: Just overnight.
Liam wants to see me.

MANI (*a voicenote*). So… yeah so the thing is, I might have
an actual date on Saturday night, like a real grown-up date
in a restaurant – I know, fucking hell – so I'd kind of prefer
not to commit to anything overnight in case it goes well? It's
probably pointless knowing my luck but… Shit is that bad?
You can say if it's bad.

David: You can bring him back here

Mani: I'm not getting arse juice
on Jill's bed!

David: Don't worry. I'll go home.

Mani: Sure?

David: I actually feel like chaos.

Bit of a pause.

Mani: Don't worry I'll do it. I'll postpone.

David: You don't have to.

Mani: I know x

Scene: Liam Meets Mani

Day. Lounge. It's raining outside. DAVID *and Liam have just had sex. They are half-dressed in different ways. Liam laughs in light exasperation.*

LIAM. We don't need to talk about it anymore!

DAVID. Okay. (*Pause.*) But you can see that it's really weird. You can't be silent for two weeks and then text me 'hi how's your week been'

LIAM. So you don't mean it's weird, you mean it's annoying.

DAVID *laughs.*

What's weird is talking about it.

DAVID. Why?

LIAM. It just is.

DAVID. I get attached very quickly.

LIAM. Don't tell me that!

DAVID. Why?

LIAM. Look… I want to be able to have sex, with someone decent enough that I can be dirty without feeling… dirty. If that makes sense. When both people feel like it. And then space when they don't.

DAVID. Okay.

LIAM. Cool.

DAVID. So you just want sex.

LIAM. Like… yeah.

A beat.

DAVID. But if you only want sex. Why with me?

LIAM. Oh my god! (Beat) I think you're sound. Is that good enough?

DAVID *is laughing.*

Do you want to watch something? Have you got time?

DAVID. Yeah. I actually can't believe how good that felt.

LIAM. I said you should try it didn't I. My god. I'm fucking hollow now.

He stands up to look for something.

Where's your remote?

DAVID. On my phone

LIAM. Look… Sometimes I'm not good at being in touch. Okay. (*A concession.*) Sorry.

A key in the front door. LIAM *does his jeans up very hastily and manages to help* DAVID *get his T-shirt on.* MANI *comes in, rain running off him.*

MANI. Hello hello.

LIAM. Alright mate.

MANI (*gruffly masculine.*) 'Alright mate'. Hello babe I'm Mani.

LIAM. Liam, nice one.

LIAM *wipes a hand on his jeans and offers it.* MANI *goes in for an air kiss.*

I'm a… friend of David's.

MANI. Well that's a fucking relief isn't it I thought you were a burglar. You're very healthy looking aren't you. He's very healthy isn't he. I bet you can get a stiff jam-jar open without a tea towel.

LIAM. Sorry what was your name?

MANI. Mani. He-him. Or they. Or her holiness. If you like.

LIAM. Oh. Right. Are you um…

DAVID. No.

MANI. I might be. (To David) I don't tell you everything. (beat) I do actually. Nah it's him that was born in the wrong body.

DAVID *laughs.*

LIAM. Don't say that!

MANI. No you're right, 'wrong body' it's very two thousand and fucking six isn't it.

LIAM. Doesn't seem very nice.

DAVID. I actually would change it if I could.

LIAM. You'd change your body?

DAVID. I'd get some tits and an extra dick.

MANI *and* LIAM *laugh*.

How was the protest?

MANI. Oh David it was so wet! Russell's cheap-ass mascara was all down his face. Even the weather at that embassy is homophobic. I snogged a boy from Amnesty. He's got a pierced scrotum and he lives on a canal boat. You should have come. (*To* LIAM.) Sorry I'm a bit not sober I've had four ciders and I'm only twelve.

LIAM. Nice one. (*A moment*.) Well I should be heading off.

DAVID. Don't you want to watch something?

LIAM. I should be getting on.

DAVID. Really?

MANI (*to* DAVID). Babe it's a Saturday, queers got lives.

LIAM. I'm not a 'queer'.

MANI. Well if it swims like a duck and rims like a duck it's probably a duck.

LIAM. You what?

MANI. I'm just saying you've probably got places to be. (To David) So um. Tonight. I'm going to try and write a bit of stand-up.

DAVID *is delighted*.

DAVID. That's brilliant.

MANI. Yeah well. Maybe… I was thinking about what you said innit. Anyway I'll be in my room. (*To* LIAM.) Nice to meet you babe.

MANI *goes.* LIAM *is quite weirded out by* MANI. *He starts putting his shoes on.*

DAVID. Are you alright?

LIAM. Yeah why? (*Beat.*) So is he like a proper mate. Or a house mate or…

DAVID. He's my best friend. He's staying here for a couple of days.

LIAM. Okay. Cool. Well I'll see you yeah?

DAVID. Will you?

LIAM. Won't I?

DAVID. What's wrong.

LIAM. Nothing. Look, do you want to do something. Like, a thing. Sometime. Something that's not here.

DAVID. A date.

LIAM. No not a date. Just –

DAVID. A drink.

LIAM. A day out.

DAVID *reacts physically with excitement.*

DAVID. I would absolutely love that.

LIAM. Okay.

DAVID. Where?

LIAM. I dunno. Can you go on trains?

DAVID. No.

LIAM. Oh.

DAVID. I'm not allowed on them.

LIAM. What?

DAVID. I'm banned from using the whole network.

LIAM. That's… dreadful.

DAVID. Not as dreadful as what I did in the buffet car.

    LIAM *realises* DAVID *is joking*.

LIAM. You prick. Well. Let's think of somewhere… accessible. Or we can just go somewhere in London. Where you haven't been.

DAVID. Out of London.

LIAM. Yeah. Fresh air. Somewhere nice. Or whatever.

DAVID. I'll have a think.

LIAM. I'll have a think too. (*Beat.*) Okay well. (*Beat.*) Cool.

    He stands there a moment. Then goes. We hear the front door. DAVID *is manically happy.*

Scene: Independence

DEREK *and* DAVID *in the living room.* DEREK *is looking at something on his phone.*

DEREK. 'Walks and Wheelchairs.'

DAVID. Liam found it.

DEREK. This is the website I showed you last year. You said it was patronising.

DAVID (*shaking his head in dismissal*). We're going to Sussex. Near Horsham.

DEREK. You should go to Brighton.

DAVID. No.

DEREK. Seems appropriate.

DAVID. Why?

DEREK. You know.

DAVID. The weather's going to be brilliant. He's quite outdoorsy. He's going to bring a picnic.

DEREK. He knows he's got to help you?

DAVID. There's a bit of forest. And a river.

DEREK. When's your train tomorrow – what time should we leave here?

DAVID. You don't need to come.

DEREK. No I know, just to get you to Victoria.

DAVID. I can do that myself.

DEREK. Well I'm meant to be working anyway so I might as well –

DAVID. I don't need you. I'll get there myself.

DEREK. Right.

DAVID. You can have the day off.

DEREK. Right. But have you got a back-up plan?

DAVID. Jill's going to be here in the evening.

DEREK. Okay but… (*Pause*.) It would have been good to know earlier. That's all.

DAVID. Sorry. It's nice to be spontaneous sometimes. It's what people do.

Text Conversation: Liam

Dark stage. A phone alarm-clock sound beeps for a while till it's cut off. A text or WhatsApp window onscreen. A chat with Liam.

8.10 a.m.

David: Hi babe.
Gorgeous day.

8.25 a.m.

David: All good?

Liam: Hey all good.

A gentle swell of noises from a railway station. Slow fade up of lights on DAVID *in his wheelchair. Texting.*

9.41 a.m.

> David: I'm really early but the train is here so
> I'm going to get a space.
> Perfect weather.

9.55 a.m.

> David: I'm on the train.
> 2nd coach
> 2nd from concourse end
> I'm the guy with the wheelchair 😊

10.02 a.m.

> David: Where are you it's going in 2 mins
> ?

The sound of automatic doors closing. DAVID *starts twitching uncontrollably.*

> David: LIAM

The sound of a train gently accelerating.

> David: the train has left
> I'm on the train
> Couldn't get off in time
> Guard didn't understand

10.05 a.m.

> Liam: Sorry fell asleep again.

> David: What the fuck????

> Liam: oh fuck just read these.

> David: I'm a fucking prisoner
> What the fuck
> Help.
> I want some water

> Liam: Are you ok

> David: I'll need a piss soon
> No.

> Liam: Fuck.

ANNOUNCER. We will shortly be arriving at Clapham
Junction.

A train slowing, stopping. Doors open.

10.09 a.m.

> David: Clapham Junction
> I'm at Clapham Junction now.

>> Liam: get off
>> Can you get off?
>>   ?

Doors closing. Train leaves the station.

> David: Help!

> What the fuck.

>> Liam: Are you at Clapham.

> David: No!
> Too late!
> I need the fucking toilet
> Where the fuck am I going

>> Liam: ?

A few moments.

>> Liam: David?
>> Why did you get on the train
>> without me?

> David: ?

>> Liam: ?
>> Why did you get on the train??

*Sound engulfs him louder and louder, until sound and lights
cut off abruptly, leaving the question on the screen a little
longer.*

Interval.

ACT TWO

Scene: Aftermath

DAVID*'s lounge*. DAVID, JILL, DEREK. DAVID *agitated, trying to speak*.

JILL. Gatwick! I thought you were with him?

DEREK. Didn't want me cramping your style, did you buddy!

JILL. Oh for God's sake! David.

DEREK. Told me to stand down.

JILL (*to* Derek). You shouldn't have.

DAVID. You're not his boss! (*Beat*.) It was supposed to be a date. Not 'take your puppy to work' day.

DEREK. Well it's all okay now. I got to him quite quickly.

JILL. Thank God. It's very kind of you.

DEREK. Well... I could do with the work.

Beat.

JILL. You're reckless.

DAVID. Calm down. I get trains by myself all the time.

JILL. But that's planned. And there's always someone at the other end. (*Warmly*.) I'm so sorry, baby. At least you didn't end up at the coast.

DEREK. I did say, we could have gone anyway. Me and him. Got ourselves onto the next train, have a day in Brighton. Couple of hours on the front.

DAVID. No.

DEREK. Get some chips.

JILL (*to* DAVID). So... you'd agreed a specific train?

DEREK. Could have had an ice cream.

JILL. You'd arranged to meet, at the station and get that specific train.

DAVID. Yeah.

DEREK. I haven't had an ice cream in about three years.

JILL. Derek, Christ's sake, I will give you two quid you can go and get yourself a bloody Magnum. (*To* DAVID.) When did you arrange all this?

DAVID. It's not 'all this', it's a day trip. (*Beat*.) A few days ago.

JILL. And he was still up for it yesterday?

DAVID. What do you mean?

JILL. As in, you spoke to him. Texted with him last night.

DAVID. I didn't talk to him yesterday.

JILL. Right. Don't you think that's weird?

DAVID. He doesn't do texting. He said some bullshit about not being very good at communicating.

JILL. It's just, most people would sort of check in the evening before. To confirm.

DAVID. It was confirmed.

JILL. Yeah but people are flaky. And they expect others to be flaky. If you hadn't spoken in a few days he probably thought it was off.

DAVID. That's insane. Why are you blaming me for this?

JILL. I'm not.

DAVID. It's his responsibility to cancel if we made a plan.

JILL. But is what I'm saying genuinely news to you?

DAVID. No.

JILL. So why didn't you check with him? (*Beat*.) David.

Pause.

DAVID. Because I didn't want to give him the chance to back out.

A moment.

DEREK. You know what, it's a lovely day, I think I might get a Magnum if you can spare me five minutes?

DAVID. Yeah.

DEREK. Great. (*He makes to go.*) I'll get us all one, eh?

JILL *fishes a note out from her purse.*

JILL. You know what, I will.

DEREK *really wants to take the note but stops himself.*

DEREK. Don't be daft, my shout.

JILL. Take it.

DEREK. Alright. Thanks. Back in five.

DEREK *goes out of the room.* JILL *points after him.*

DAVID. What?

JILL. He's broke. He was probably counting on a day's work today.

DEREK *comes back in. It's unclear if he's heard this.*

DEREK. Sorry. What do you want?

JILL. Anything. Nothing minty.

DEREK. Great, cheers.

He goes.

JILL. I hope you're going to pay him.

DAVID. Thank you. I know I have to pay people to help me!

JILL. He's probably had to cancel whatever plans he had.

DAVID. Of course I'll pay him.

DEREK *comes back in.*

DEREK. What if they've only got mint?

JILL. Burn the fucking shop down.

DEREK. Right, yeah. Cheers.

    DEREK *goes*.

JILL. I just don't understand why you got on the train.

DAVID. I didn't think he was a cunt.

    We hear the outside door close.

JILL. Baby, people let people down all the time. It's like you set this up to fail.

DAVID. Why would I do that?

JILL. I don't know. (*Beat*.) Derek shouldn't have let you do this.

DAVID. I'm his boss.

JILL. Yes, I know. But this need to do everything on your own terms.

DAVID. Like an adult?

JILL. I was saying to Michael. These risks – all these men coming here.

DAVID. It would be just as risky if you had random men back here.

JILL. I don't. (*Pause*.) I just wonder if it's worth talking to your social worker.

DAVID. What the fuck?!

JILL. Not behind your back. They could be more hands-on.

DAVID. I'm twenty-five.

JILL. Sort some proper… assistants. From an agency.

DAVID. Oh great! Two hours a day, rest of the time in nappies, won't put me on the toilet for a piss without installing a fucking hoist.

JILL. Well, technically you're meant to have a hoist.

DAVID. It's my flat. They refuse to try to understand my voice.

JILL. I just don't want you to be unsafe.

DAVID. That's my right! If you talk to them I will never talk to you again.

JILL. Wow. I'm just trying to be a friend.

DAVID. Don't talk to them.

JILL. I won't. I'm sorry I said anything. Okay?

DAVID. Yeah.

JILL. Okay?

DAVID. Yeah.

JILL. You've nothing to prove.

DAVID. I have. What a prospect. A boy who can't even go on a date by himself.

JILL. You knew he might not be reliable.

DAVID. I didn't. I thought he was perfect. He is perfect. I don't know.

JILL. He's got mental health issues. I'm not criticising I'm just saying.

DAVID. He gets a bit down.

JILL. He goes days without talking to anyone, he's got what sounds like quite serious body issues. I'm just…

Pause. She steels herself.

I know this is a big… thing for you. A very… attractive, nice man clearly likes you. But well – oh god please don't take this the wrong way but you're a challenge. You're brilliant, but you're a challenge. And someone with a hot body *and* a completely sorted life is probably just not going to go for you.

DAVID *reacts physically to this, like he's been hit.*

I'm sorry. Something's got to give. And I think what's important is that if you are going to be with someone, the important thing, is that they are sorted. It's not going to be perfect and if you pretend it is… (*Pause.*) Sorry I've lost my thread a bit.

Long pause.

DAVID. Is that why you've got a gay boyfriend?

JILL. Oh fuck off. (*Pause.*) Everyone's a bit bi these days, you've said it yourself.

DAVID. I'm not.

JILL. Or pansexual. He's just very honest and secure.

DAVID. A lot of gay men had girlfriends first.

JILL. He's not gay. He goes down on me, enthusiastically. It's like being fracked. (*Beat.*) Just because you fancy him.

DAVID. I fancy everyone. No, I don't.

Pause.

JILL. So how have you left it? With Liam.

DAVID. I told him I'd pissed myself.

JILL. Well that's going to keep him keen.

DAVID. I don't want to keep him keen. I told him never to speak to me again. Fuck. Am I stupid?

JILL (*gently*). No. Of course not. (*Decisive.*) Come on. You invited me to help you salvage this lovely sunny day and here we are cooped up in the shade waiting for what I'm increasingly nervous is going to be a mint fucking Magnum. If he brings me a Mini Milk I'll scream. Let's go to the park. Derek can meet us there. Yeah?

DAVID *just sits there.*

David?

Eventually, DAVID *nods.*

Dating App Chat: SaneSorted

SaneSorted: Hi how's it going?

David: I'm looking for someone to wank me off. I have cerebral palsy and can't do it myself.

SaneSorted: Nice to meet you too lol

David: Sorry!
I have been trying for ages. I'm very tired.

SaneSorted: No worries 👍

David: How are you?
Pause.

David: ?
Pause.

David: You up for it?

Dating App Chat: Paolo

Paolo: Sounds good

David: [Sends location].

Paolo: I can come tomorrow?

David: No
I don't want to plan ahead

Paolo: Horny haha

David: People cancel. Or disappear.

Paolo: I won't baby 😘

David: You did last time we chatted

The chat vanishes. Paolo has blocked him.

Scene: Alan's Meat

On screen, the name 'ALAN' appears briefly.

Living room. DAVID *is in his wheelchair. Standing facing him is* ALAN. ALAN *has greasy, unruly hair; ill-fitting clothes; red blotches on his face. His posture emphasises his paunch. His scruffy coat resembles a school anorak and he has a supermarket carrier bag in his hand. As he talks, he puts the bag down and removes his coat, revealing a sweat-stained shirt. He's nervous, and covers it with a kind of bravado.*

ALAN. You were lucky I was nearby. I'm not usually around here. Is this your own place then?

DAVID. Yeah.

ALAN *takes it in but makes no observations.*

ALAN. So yes you were lucky really. Can I put some meat in your fridge? Before we… I don't know how long I'll be here.

DAVID. Not long.

ALAN. No I will anyway, it's reduced, little sticker on it. It's warm in here otherwise I'd risk it.

In awkward silence he takes the bag into the kitchen. We hear the fridge open and close. He returns.

You like the older man then.

DAVID. Sometimes.

Pause.

ALAN. Now, where do you want me?

DAVID (*stalling*). Do you want a drink?

ALAN. I didn't catch that, sorry. Bedroom, is it?

DAVID. Do – you – want – a – drink?

ALAN. Oh. Okay yes. If you like. There's no rush is there. Cup of tea, or just water, that's fine. It's warm out there – have you been out, do you go out?

DAVID. Yeah.

ALAN. I'm quite sweaty, I'm a bit overdressed… It was cloudier when I left the house. I'll just take some water.

Pause.

DAVID. I can't get it for you.

ALAN. Oh. No.

ALAN goes to the kitchen, and we hear the appropriate sounds.

(*Off.*) So you can't sort yourself out you were saying?

DAVID. No.

ALAN returns.

ALAN. Funny tap you've got. If you don't mind me asking, how long has it been.

DAVID. Five days.

ALAN. You'll be bursting, lad your age. Where shall we go. In here? Shall we draw the curtains.

DAVID. I'm actually quite tired.

ALAN. Well it's a warm day. (*Beat.*) We don't need to go crazy.

DAVID. I'm sorry. I didn't realise how tired I was. I didn't mean to waste your time.

ALAN. You're not wasting my time!

DAVID's movements become quite stressed and pronounced. ALAN realises this isn't happening.

Oh. Right, I see. Yes, no that's alright. No I, I should probably be getting on with things.

DAVID. I'm just tired. Sorry.

ALAN. Course. (*He gets his jacket.*) Okay. See you.

ALAN goes into the hall, puts his head back into the room.

How do I…?

DAVID. Push the bar.

We hear ALAN leaving, a brief burst of sound from outside, the door closing. DAVID relaxes a bit. Then the doorbell goes once, twice. DAVID *presses a button on a keyfob. We hear the door open.*

ALAN (*off*). I forgot my meat.

ALAN *enters, nods awkwardly, goes to the kitchen and retrieves his bag of meat. He loiters.*

It can just be a wank. If that's more what you're looking for… A quick one. (*Long pause.*) I mean I'm here now. And it's been five days, has it?

Pause.

DAVID. Okay.

ALAN. Yes?

Pause.

DAVID. Yeah.

Dating App Chat: Hole4U

Hole4U: U host

David: Yes

Hole4U: Free now

David: Wait lol. I have cerebral palsy
[sends more obviously 'disabled' pic]
I use a wheelchair

Pause.

Never mind

Pause.

?

Hole4U: Another time

David: I have a really big dick

Hole4U: Where are you?

Scene: David and Nuno

On screen, the name 'NUNO' appears briefly.

NUNO *is straddling* DAVID, *who is on his back. He's younger than the other one-off hook-ups. He has a Portuguese or Spanish accent.*

NUNO. Yes you sexy.

> NUNO *licks his hand, gets plenty of spit on it. He reaches behind him to lube* DAVID's *dick up.*

DAVID. Get a condom.

> NUNO *lets a smile play over his lips. Has he heard?*

Get a condom.

NUNO. You want to fill my hole, baby?

DAVID. Get a condom.

> NUNO *pushes* DAVID's *dick inside him, pressing down to take him all in. Moans happily.*

I said get a condom!

NUNO. I did not understand your voice.

DAVID. You did.

> NUNO *starts riding* DAVID.

Stop!

NUNO. No. Ssh.

DAVID. Yes. Stop!

NUNO. It's so good, baby. You feel so good.

DAVID. Get off!

NUNO. You are hard. You like it.

> DAVID's *body is reacting quite severely.*

It's okay. I am on PrEP

DAVID. I'm not. Stop!

NUNO *puts a hand over* DAVID*'s mouth.*

NUNO. Sshhh it's good.

NUNO *keeps riding him.* DAVID *shouts through* NUNO*'s hand.*

DAVID. Get off!

NUNO. When you last come?

DAVID. What?

NUNO *stops moving.*

NUNO. When did you last come?

DAVID. A few days ago.

NUNO. A few days?

DAVID. Yeah.

NUNO. Good.

NUNO *starts riding him again.*

DAVID. Get off!

NUNO *stops. A moment.*

NUNO. You want to come?

DAVID. Yeah.

NUNO. You want to spunk?

DAVID. Yes.

NUNO. Then you fuck me bare like this. Or I don't make you come.

Text Conversation: Mani

David: Hi

Deletes, writes again, sends.

Mani: Heyyyyyyy

Pause.

David: how are u

Mani: getting ready

mate's bday

u ok?

Pause.

David: yeah

Text conversation: Dad

Dad: Don't forget it's your
mum's birthday on Thursday.
Hope you're well.
Dad.

David (*starts to type*): Yes I

Deletes. Starts to type.

I know

Deletes.

thanks

Starts to type.

I'm ok

Deletes.

Scene: A Smashing Time

DAVID *is sat on his bed, looking at something on his phone.
Next to the bed on a little table is a glass of water, and his
terrarium. He's in a dark mood.* DEREK *comes in with a tea
towel.*

DEREK. Do you want a drink, buddy?

DAVID. No.

DEREK. Anything else?

DAVID. No. Thank you.

Pause.

DEREK. Well I might just run through my audition bits till my time's up.

DAVID. Okay.

DEREK. I'll be in there then.

> DEREK *hovers. There's a T-shirt crumpled on the floor. He picks it up, wonders what to do with it. Puts it in a laundry basket. He hovers again.*

It's a new play, this one. (*Beat.*) A lot of typos.

DAVID. You can go home if you want.

DEREK. Don't be daft.

DAVID. Jill's in.

DEREK. I know but… she's in her room with Michael. I'll do till ten.

DAVID. I'll pay you the full shift.

DEREK. Okay. Thanks, buddy.

> DEREK *goes. We hear the front door close. After a while* DAVID *looks to where his glass stands on a table or chest of drawers. It has a straw in it. On his knees,* DAVID *awkwardly goes over to it. He reaches for it but because of his movements he knocks it off and it breaks on the floor.*

DAVID. FUCK. FUCK. (*Beat.*) FUCK. (*Beat.*) Jill! Jill! (*He summons more energy.*) Jill!!

> *He kicks about, making noise. A few seconds later,* JILL *bursts into the room.*

JILL. Oh my god.

> *She kneels beside him.*

DAVID. I can't get up.

JILL. What's happened? Oh god there's glass. Stay still.

DAVID. I can't stay fucking still.

JILL. Are you hurt?

DAVID. No.

JILL. Let me help you. Careful.

She helps him up, and onto the mattress. MICHAEL *enters in his underwear.*

MICHAEL. Dude?

DAVID. I'm fine.

MICHAEL. There's glass on the floor.

MICHAEL *kneels to start picking it up.*

DAVID. Leave it.

JILL. Don't be silly.

DAVID. Go away!

MICHAEL *stops, raises his hands in silent appeasement, stands up.*

JILL. Give me a minute.

MICHAEL *goes.*

(*To* DAVID.) Wait there.

She exits. We hear clattering. She comes back with a dustpan and brush, and starts sweeping glass into it.

Where's Derek?

DAVID. I sent him home.

JILL *puts the dustpan down.*

JILL. Why?

DAVID. I'm fine.

JILL. Clearly.

DAVID. I can't cope any more.

JILL. What?

DAVID. I can't cope.

JILL. You'll be okay.

DAVID. I wish I'd never gone on Grindr. It's Pandora's box. Pandora's cunt. I'm so fucking naive.

JILL. In the last few months you've had sex with more people than I've had in my life.

DAVID. Liam was the one.

JILL. My love, every time some guys sucks you off for five minutes they're the one.

DAVID. This is different. He was like real life. Like other people's real life! (*Pause*.) No wonder he went quiet after we first met. 'Thanks for the hot sex last night can you put me on the toilet now.' How fucking glamorous. I'm worthless. I can't even hold a glass of water. I'm just a fetish puppet for old men to wank off. How fucking disgusting.

JILL. You rave about your older men.

DAVID. Of course I rave about them. It doesn't sound so tragic that way.

JILL. You can't measure yourself by who you date.

DAVID. Can you actually fucking listen to me? It's different. I'm different!

JILL. You met Liam, you'll meet others.

DAVID. Not good ones! You said that!

JILL. I didn't say that. 'Good ones.'

DAVID. You did and you were right. Why should they put up with a useless shitty fucking savage crawling stunted cripple.

JILL. Darling –

DAVID. An animal. A fucking crude, unfinished, unrefined animal. I should get castrated.

It takes JILL *a moment to find any words.*

JILL. Has – has something happened?

DAVID *shakes his head.*

DAVID. Right! Let's try again! Can you get me another glass?

JILL. Um… Shall we clear this one up first.

DAVID. Who's 'we'. (*Beat.*) Please get me a glass now.

Pause. JILL *gets up, exits, returns with a glass of water with a straw in it.*

Empty it.

JILL. Empty it?

DAVID. I want an empty glass.

JILL, *nonplussed, goes out and returns with the empty glass.*

Put it on the table.

JILL. What are we doing?

DAVID. Put it on the table.

JILL. You don't need to do this.

DAVID. It's important!

JILL. Why don't you try with something plastic?

DAVID. Because I'm not a toddler! Put the glass on the table.

JILL. This is pointless.

DAVID. I want to fill a glass with water and drink it like a normal person.

JILL. Why?

DAVID. So that I don't feel like a fucking imbecile, you fucking cunt.

Stunned, JILL *puts the glass on the table next to the terrarium. She sits down.*

JILL. David, I know this isn't the moment but I think… I think I should move out.

DAVID. Don't be dramatic.

JILL. I've been thinking about it for a while.

DAVID. You want to move in with Michael.

JILL. No. (*Beat.*) Not necessarily. I'm finally starting to be out of the woods a bit, financially, and…

DAVID. You don't need me so you're fucking off.

JILL. I'm your friend, David. Our friendship matters a lot to me. It's going to get broken if I stay here, with all that that brings with it.

DAVID. Bye then.

JILL. I'll wait as long as it takes you to find someone. Maybe Mani would want to… But don't you think?

DAVID. No.

JILL. It's just very… unequal.

DAVID. Yes. You're not fucking disabled.

A moment. He reaches for the glass as she watches, silent. Struggling, he lunges, bringing both the glass and the terrarium down. The latter falls to pieces as it hits the floor. JILL wants to react, hurt, but stops herself. DAVID suddenly starts beating his hands onto the glass on the floor, out of control, his fists bloodying. JILL pulls him away – he resists at first. Then sobs. She holds him.

Go away.

JILL. The first-aid kit. I'll get Michael.

DAVID. No!

JILL. I'll get it then.

DAVID. Go away.

JILL. I'll get it.

She stands and leaves the room.

Dating App Chat: Deo

> Deo: Come to mine if you want

David: Can you come to mine?

> Deo: I don't want to go out
> It's raining

David: It's easier

> Deo: You can come here or not
> it's up to you

David: Have you got level access

> Deo: ?

David: for my wheelchair

> Deo: Oh. No.
> Stairs.
> Sorry! 🌑

Scene: Michael Pops Round for Something

DAVID *is on his phone. His computer is on nearby, he's been writing some kind of document.*

MICHAEL. You on your own, are you?

DAVID. Yeah. Mani's at work. Derek's at Sainsbury's.

MICHAEL. I'm not disturbing, am I?

DAVID. No. Jill said you were coming.

MICHAEL. Right, yeah. So she said she's got like a griddle pan here? She wants it tonight but she's stuck at the shop so I said I'd get it… That's okay, is it?

DAVID. Yeah.

MICHAEL *goes into the kitchen and rummages.*

MICHAEL (*off*). How's it going anyway, man?

DAVID. Okay.

MICHAEL (*off*). Yeah?

DAVID. I'm writing a pitch for an article.

MICHAEL (*off*). Oh yeah? (*Beat.*) I don't really know what I'm looking for in here. Do you?

DAVID. I haven't done any cooking since I won the *Bake Off*.

MICHAEL. You what? Oh *Bake Off*, haha nice one. (*He emerges.*) I think this is it. With the ridges. (*Beat.*) She says hi.

> MICHAEL *notices that* DAVID *is typing on his phone.*

You're glued to that thing, aren't you.

DAVID. I can't type much on the computer. Derek types for me.

MICHAEL. I'm not criticising. No I think it's brilliant. God it must have been so hard being disabled before smartphones! When you think about it.

DAVID. I'm actually on Grindr.

MICHAEL. Oh yeah?

> MICHAEL *has a look over* DAVID's *shoulder.*

Amazing! Right well I'll… (*Pause.*) Do you need anything? A tea or anything?

DAVID. I've actually got a guy about to come round.

MICHAEL. Have you?!

DAVID. He's actually very hot. Look at him.

> MICHAEL *looks.*

MICHAEL. Wow, dude. Get you.

DAVID. He's probably high.

MICHAEL. What do you mean?

DAVID. The hot ones always are.

MICHAEL. Oh.

*DAVID scrolls up through a chat on his phone then laughs.
MICHAEL looks at why.*

Fuck, he's quite a big lad, isn't he.

DAVID. That's mine. (*He laughs.*) Sorry.

MICHAEL is quite flustered.

MICHAEL. No, er… (*Beat.*) Well, he'll have a good time.

DAVID. He should be here by now.

MICHAEL. Well I'll get out of your hair, if you'll excuse the
pun.

DAVID. What pun?

MICHAEL. You know, like there's come in your hair… or
something… it's not really a pun. Have you got a carrier
bag?

DAVID. In the kitchen.

MICHAEL. Sweet.

*MICHAEL goes into the kitchen and rummages. Meanwhile
on the screen we see an app chat:*

David: Are you lost?

Malfoy: Sorry man still at home.

David: Ok

Malfoy: Sorry man let's take a rain check
yeah? Tomorrow

David: No! I need to cum.
Now.

Malfoy: Haha you'll find someone

David: Three people have fucking cancelled. I
need to wank.
Please.
Please come.

The conversation disappears. He's been blocked.

DAVID. Fuck!! (*He flings his phone down*.) FUCK.

MICHAEL *returns from the kitchen*.

MICHAEL. Hey. What's wrong? You alright?

DAVID. Selfish cunt.

MICHAEL *is a bit freaked by how angry* DAVID *is at this*.

MICHAEL. Okay… well there's plenty more I bet.

DAVID. I haven't come in a week.

MICHAEL. Is that long? Monks go years, don't they.

DAVID. That's a choice! Can you imagine. What it is like.
Every time you want to just spunk and get on with your life
you have to wait for someone to turn up. Four men have
cancelled in a row. I can't fucking stand it any more! I get
so excited. It's like being in a chastity belt. I need help to
eat. Fine. I need help to shit. Fine. But begging for a fucking
wank. It is so fucking degrading. I'm so tired.

Beat.

MICHAEL. I'm sorry, man.

DAVID. All I need is someone to jerk my dick for five minutes.

MICHAEL. So he was literally just going to wank you off?

DAVID. I don't know. But that's all it needs to be. (*Beat*.) I'm
meant to be writing a pitch. To the fucking *Observer*. They
liked the idea. They might even pay me. And all I can think
about is my cock. (*With meaning*.) Anyone could do it.

Beat.

MICHAEL. So they wouldn't even… like they wouldn't even
have to… get involved. Apart from. Doing that… Just a five-
minute… wank.

DAVID. Yeah. Not even five probably.

MICHAEL. That's all you'd need?

DAVID. Yeah.

A moment.

MICHAEL. Is here alright?

DAVID. Yeah.

MICHAEL *goes to* DAVID. *He undoes his jeans, struggling a little with the button.* DAVID *gasps as* MICHAEL*'s hands reach for his dick and starts jerking him.* DAVID *can't speak.*

MICHAEL. This okay?

DAVID *signals that it is.* MICHAEL *gets more into it. His other hand goes to his own crotch, feeling himself through his jeans. He wrestles with a thought for a moment – then goes with it, bending to put his mouth to* DAVID*'s dick.* DAVID *moans in pleasure.*

He doesn't hear the front door open, and moans again loudly. MICHAEL *hears it close, panics, sees that the door to the hall is open and rushes to it to slam it closed before returning to* DAVID.

DEREK *enters as* MICHAEL *is starting to try and do* DAVID*'s jeans up, not helped by* DAVID, *who is squirming from panic and frustration. A moment of awkward realisation.*

Hey.

DEREK. Hey…

MICHAEL *looks for and grabs the griddle pan.*

MICHAEL. Jill wanted her griddle pan. This is it, yeah?

DEREK. Yeah.

MICHAEL *waits for* DEREK *to leave the room. He doesn't.*

MICHAEL. Sweet. Well I'll see you, mate, yeah?

DAVID. Yeah.

MICHAEL (*re: the griddle pan*). Cheers for this.

MICHAEL *leaves.* DEREK *is clearly troubled.*

DAVID. Don't tell her.

DEREK. It's not very nice, buddy.

DAVID. It's none of your business.

DEREK. What if she finds out?

DAVID. Don't tell her!

DEREK. From *him*. What if *he* feels guilty and tells her? Maybe you should tell her. (*Beat.*) They were out of the usual pasta bakes. I got tuna.

DAVID. Can you do my trousers up.

DEREK *nods, and goes to him to fix his jeans.*

DEREK. It just isn't very fair.

DAVID. Nothing's fair.

DEREK. No, well, it's not very fair on me, knowing my friend's boyfriend is a cheat and not being able to tell her.

DAVID. Don't be dramatic. She's not your friend.

DEREK. She is!

DAVID. Only through me. You don't even know what he's allowed to actually do.

DEREK. Then it doesn't matter if she knows does it.

DAVID. I will fire you if you tell her. You only saw it because you're my assistant. Not my friend. A friend wouldn't just walk into my flat. You are my arms, my fingers, my legs. When you are here you are me.

DEREK. I see.

DAVID. You're not my conscience. You're not my buddy. Do you call Jill 'buddy'?

DEREK. No, but –

DAVID. No cos it's fucking patronising.

Pause.

It was just a wank.

DEREK. So you think you've done nothing wrong.

DAVID. Of course I have. Of course it was wrong. Don't tell her.

Voicemail Messages: Jill and Trish

JILL (*on voicemail*). Hello, this is David's phone. Please don't call back or leave a message. Text or email instead. Thank you.

TRISH (*on voicemail*). Hello, David! It's Trish at the *Observer*, got the latest email, I think that all sounds really interesting! Let's do it. Drop me a line and we'll sort the details. Looking forward to it.

Scene: David's Dad Visits

Late evening. Living room. DAVID*'s dad is with* DAVID. *He has an overnight bag. He helps* DAVID *take off his coat, pulling over his arms and head.*

DAD. Is Jill off doing something nice?

DAVID. Yeah.

DAD. Mani's holding the fort again, is he?

DAVID. He'll be back soon.

DAD. You should have told him, he doesn't need to stay tonight.

DAVID. I thought we were only going to meet for dinner. I didn't think you'd be staying over.

DAD. Well it'll be very nice to meet him.

DAVID. You got a hotel last time.

DAD. I was *speaking* at that conference so they paid for the room. Anyway I thought this might be… I mean, I do pay for the flat! (*Beat.*) I thought we might have a chat.

DAVID. We have been chatting.

DAD. Alright, well, a different chat… Would you like a drink? I might have a cup of tea.

DAVID. Beer.

DAD. Tea.

DAVID. *I'll* have a beer. They're in the fridge.

DAD. Oh. Right-oh. I might have one as well.

He goes to the kitchen and returns with two beers. One with a straw. He gives DAVID *some.*

We're just bit…

DAVID. What?

DAD. Don't take this the wrong way, please, but when you told us you were gay it was like finding out your blood type. It didn't seem like a thing that would have much bearing. Your mother's vague about it but it sounds like you have stranger after stranger in your home.

DAVID. Would you say that if I wasn't disabled?

DAD. Don't do that with me. A lot of things would be very different if you weren't disabled.

DAVID. Mum told me that one of her biggest fears for me when I was little was that I'd never have sexual fulfilment.

DAD. Did she?

DAVID. You must know.

DAD. I suppose. No. We didn't really talk about that.

DAVID. You must have thought about it.

DAD nods.

I'm a sexual being, Dad.

DAD. Everyone is. Of course.

DAVID. *I* am.

DAD. I know that. Don't I?! I had to wipe you up sometimes. In the mornings. When you woke up.

DAVID laughs, a little, at this. Pause.

I'm not judging you I just, it's very different to what we – I – imagined. Would imagine for anyone.

We watched a thing, ITV I think, a real-life drama - this man who killed young gay men with something. GMB? No.

DAVID. GHB.

DAD. Right.

DAVID. Where the fuck are you going with this? I don't take GHB.

DAD. Well I don't know what you do.

DAVID. It's none of your business.

DAD. Well you clearly think it's your mother's business.

They're interrupted by the sound of the front door. They stay quiet until MANI speaks.

MANI *(off)*. Hiyaaaaa! Oh my lordy lord, David, what a ridiculous evening. You here?

MANI bursts into the room.

Fucking – Oh! Sorry didn't know you were having someone round. Should have guessed! *(To DAD.)* Only joking, he's a virgin, go easy on him. Hello, I'm Mani.

DAD. ...Tim. Timothy.

MANI. Just going to get some water and I'll be out of here.

MANI goes into the kitchen. Runs a tap. DAVID and DAD are nearly dying with embarrassment.

(Off.) Can I get you anything?

DAD. No thank you.

MANI. David?

MANI *returns with a glass of water.*

DAVID. No. This is my dad.

MANI *absorbs this with horror and remembers something.*

MANI. The conference! (*Wildly improvising.*) I hope they do you a good buffet! That's the best bit. I'll be – I'll leave you to it.

MANI *exits, we can hear him say 'fuck' once he's out of the room. A long silence while* DAD *helps* DAVID *drink from his beer.* DAVID *nods when he's had enough.*

DAD. I could pay for him to get a taxi home if he doesn't want to stay here tonight. I'll take his bed.

DAVID. He lives here.

DAD. What do you mean?

DAVID. Jill moved out.

DAD. When? Why?!

DAVID. She got a fucking boyfriend.

DAD. Oh. Good for her. Why didn't you… Is Mani, um…

DAVID. You can say gay.

DAD. No not that, come on, why would I… No, is he responsible?

DAVID. He's brilliant.

DAD. Look, do you want to come home?

DAVID. When?

DAD. Not for a weekend. For a… a while.

DAVID *jerks, uncontrollably.*

Well that's a reaction.

DAVID. I live here.

DAD. We just thought, your mum and I...

DAVID. You do talk then.

DAD. Of course we bloody talk.

DAVID. She likes that I meet people.

DAD. Right well she's my wife, David, but what would I know.

DAVID. You wouldn't want me at home.

DAD *can't deny this.*

DAD. I... It's not about what I want. I mean of course you'd be welcome, we'd find some local assistants for you, it might be less chaotic. Is Mani always drunk?

DAVID. No!

DAD. You got rid of one housemate who was always drunk.

DAVID. Did Mum say I met someone?

DAD. She did, yes. (*Beat.*) Well that's good! Still on the scene then, is he?

DAVID. It's not a thing now, I'm just saying. I don't know why.

DAD. Look, just think about it, that's all. Coming home.

DAVID. I've got commitments.

DAD. I'm sure they have community websites you could help out with at home. Think about it.

DAVID. No.

DAD. As an option. If you need some time out. A chance to reset.

DAVID. Okay.

DAD. Okay?

DAVID. I'll think about it.

DAD *nods. A moment.*

DAD. Your cousin's back home. He quit uni.

DAVID. Why?

DAD. I don't know. Nothing in that boy's life makes sense.
Your mum thinks he got all that out of his system too young.

DAVID *laughs*.

What?

DAVID. Do you remember he was in that band?

DAD. His band! (*Laughs*.) Jo's wedding. Why would you play
heavy metal at the wedding of a woman who's so religious
she'll only go on holiday to places where apparitions of the
Virgin Mary have been sighted? (*Beat*.) His 18th birthday.

DAVID. It was like Glastonbury.

DAD. It was like one of those paintings of hell.

They both laugh. It subsides.

DAVID. I'm tired now.

DAD. I'll take the sofa, shall I?

DAVID. Yeah. Sorry.

DAD. Oh I can sleep on anything.

DAVID. Thanks for dinner.

DAD. My pleasure. (*Beat*.) Put you to bed?

DAVID. Mani can do it.

DAD. I don't mind.

DAVID. It's fine.

DAD. Let me.

DAVID. I can manage.

DAD. Okay.

DAVID. I'll get him.

*DAVID eases himself out of the chair, and walks awkwardly
on his knees to the door, and out of it. DAD swigs his beer.*

Voicenote from Liam

LIAM (a *voicenote*). Hi David, it's Liam… Hope you're doing okay. So er, I've been thinking about you quite a lot and it would be really nice to see you again, I don't know if you'd want that or… Like I totally get it if you don't but I thought I'd give you a shout. I got a bit scared I think. Sorry. Anyway yeah hope you're good. Cheers.

Text Conversation: Liam

David: Why have you been thinking about me?

Liam: You're special.
How have you been?

David: That's a big question. It has been a while.

Liam: I know.
The longer I left it the more
I didn't know how to say hi.
I fucked up.

David: Do you really want to see me?

Liam: Yes!

David: I'm having a dinner party in a couple of weeks. You will be very welcome.

Liam: I kinda meant just us

David: I'm quite busy otherwise.
It's up to you.

Scene: David Has a Dinner Party

DAVID, DEREK, LIAM *and* MANI *at a small table in the garden. They've finished eating. A sun-drenched summer evening and they're dressed for it.*

MANI. So I got four massive laughs and maybe ten polite laughs, and there was a woman on the front row who was doing this sort of very kind but nervous smile at me from start to finish... I think that's not bad? For a five-minute open-mic slot?

DEREK. Sounds like it went well to me.

DAVID. I'm sorry I missed it.

MANI. Hey, you were feeling ill.

DAVID. I wanted to heckle you.

MANI. I wanted to pick on you.

DAVID. I'd have loved that.

MANI. You might get another chance. They asked me to do a beginners' night next month. Ten minutes this time. (*Beat.*) Shall we try Jill again?

DAVID. No.

MANI. It's just a bit weird, isn't it?

DAVID. Don't know.

DEREK. Well I just think it's a pity. I made six possets.

MANI. Well it was lush, Derek, thank you.

DEREK. I'm just the paid help. Thank the host.

MANI. Well thank you, David, but thank you, Derek.

DAVID *sort of bangs on a table awkwardly.*

DEREK. You alright bud– Er, mate?

DAVID. I want to say something. I wanted to say thank you to my friends for being there for me. I don't always show how grateful I am. But I am.

MANI. Well I want to say something too. Living here for free and not being able to go out most nights, I've saved about two grand and my skin is even more beautiful than ever.

Laughter.

Seriously though, babe, you got to find someone soon, I can't do it much longer, I miss having people looking at me with concern.

LIAM. Should there be a toast?

MANI. A toast! To my friend who is a bona fide national journalist.

DAVID (*delighted*). It's only one article.

LIAM. Just a shame it's the *Observer*.

MANI. I know, man. Fucking right-wing rag. Cheers.

LIAM/DEREK. Cheers.

LIAM. So what's it about then?

DAVID. It's about the relationships between severely disabled adults and their parents. I'm interviewing people for it. One day I'll do something that isn't about fucking disability!

DEREK. You should use the garden more. It's nice for eating.

DAVID. Barbecue.

DEREK. We could do it up a bit, few plants.

MANI. We should all have more plants.

LIAM. You are so middle class!

MANI. I'm literally not middle class.

DEREK. I… probably am middle class.

MANI. No we should. They de-pollute the air.

LIAM. Isn't that forests?

DAVID. There's no soil. We could get some pots.

LIAM. You want growbags.

DEREK. Remember those?

MANI. Alright, Dad.

LIAM. I've got some.

DAVID. Have you?!

DEREK. Sweet peas.

LIAM. Tomatoes. Stand them up against the wall there.

MANI. What about dates?

LIAM. Dates?

MANI (*pointed*). Yeah, I heard you like standing dates up.

LIAM. It wasn't a date.

Pause.

DEREK. I did a play once where the whole set was a live garden. Grass, plants, the lot. It was meant to last a month, four shows in they were all dead. It kind of added something, to be honest.

MANI. I want someone to do a gay version of *Othello* called *Oh Hello!* Honestly, that was absolutely gorgeous.

LIAM. Yeah. Top nosh, mate.

MANI. I'm so hard for how straight you are.

LIAM. Fuck off.

MANI. Babe, put your big butch balls back in your loose-fitting polyester-mix M&S boxers, I'm being affectionate.

DEREK *starts clearing plates.*

DAVID. Leave that.

MANI. Yeah, relax.

DEREK. I'm just worried about wasps.

MANI. I'm worried about climate change but this weather can sit on my face. Sit down.

The doorbell goes. DEREK *stands.* MANI *stops him.*

I'll go.

MANI *goes into the house.* DAVID *looks agitated.*

LIAM. You okay?

DAVID. Yeah.

DEREK. Alright there, buddy?

DAVID *nods.* JILL *appears in the garden,* MANI *following her. She keeps her eyes on* DAVID.

JILL. Hello, everyone. Sorry I'm late. I haven't brought wine. Is there any?

LIAM *pours her a glass.*

You must be Liam.

LIAM *offers a hand. She shakes her head.*

MANI. No Michael?

JILL. That's right.

DAVID *just twitches.* JILL *lets him.*

DAVID. I'm sorry.

JILL. Speak clearly!

LIAM. Hey!

JILL. Just shut up and listen to what you're getting yourself into. (*To* DAVID.) Well?

DAVID. He was being kind.

JILL. I know, he is kind. What were *you* being? (*Beat.*) A nasty cruel selfish little troll.

DAVID. It was just a blowjob.

JILL. A blowjob! He said it was a wank!

DAVID. It was until the end.

JILL. Oh good!

DAVID. It was weeks ago.

JILL. And he told me one hour ago! I think he panicked
you'd get drunk tonight and say something. (*Beat*.) Okay.
Look, look, help me out. Can you give me some kind of
understanding as to what the fuck exactly made you think,
'Oh, it's only Jill, it doesn't matter about Jill, Jill doesn't
matter.'

DAVID. It wasn't about you.

JILL. Jesus Christ. My life has revolved around you. This was
mine. Michael was mine. And you couldn't fucking bear it,
could you?

DAVID (*barely decipherable*). He was just a hand. I was
frustrated.

JILL. I can't understand you, you fucking prick. Try harder.

DAVID. I was frustrated.

JILL. Well it hasn't worked if you were trying to ruin it. I don't
blame him. You're manipulative. He felt sorry for you. He
said it was gross!

DAVID. He didn't.

JILL. He did. Gross! I am going to email your social worker and
your parents.

DAVID. Fuck off.

JILL. You can't be trusted.

DAVID. I am not a child.

JILL. What??

DAVID. A child.

JILL. No, you're a fucking monster.

DAVID. Don't be so sheltered!

JILL. Some of us still have a vague notion of normal decent morals, David!

Pause.

DEREK. Maybe it wouldn't be a terrible idea if you started doing things more… conventionally, or if you had a bit of time back home for a while, eh? For your sake.

DAVID. Traitor!

DEREK. We care about you, David.

JILL. I don't.

DEREK. Well I do. You've got a bit lost, I think. With the… sex stuff.

DAVID. At least I have sex.

DEREK. You missed Mani's comedy gig for a hook-up.

DAVID *spasms*. MANI*'s shocked by this but he contains it.*

It's not like you.

Long pause.

MANI (*flatly*). It's fine.

DAVID. Derek.

JILL. It isn't fine.

DAVID. Derek!

MANI. Okay, well.

DAVID. Derek. Derek.

DEREK. Yes?

DAVID. I'm giving you your notice.

JILL. This is absurd.

DAVID. You're absurd. I'm giving Derek his notice. He shouldn't have told Mani that. He can't be trusted.

DEREK. That's a bit unfair. I kept the thing with Michael under wraps for you.

JILL. Oh fucking hell! (*To* MANI.) Did you know as well?
Mani? Fucking boys' club. (*To* LIAM.) What about you? Was
there a banner up? Did you see something about it on bloody
Twitter?

LIAM. I'm not on Twitter.

JILL *just stares at him.*

DEREK. It's not my job to tell you privileged information.

JILL. 'Privileged information', who are you, the civil fucking
service? It's not your job to lie for this nasty jealous pervert.

DAVID. I *was* jealous. Michael is nice. And I was angry with
you.

JILL. And you invite me to a… dinner party! So you could,
what, sit here and gloat?

DAVID. No. (*Beat.*) I invited you because I value you. (*Beat.*)
And I felt guilty.

JILL. You are fucking mental.

DAVID. I miss you.

JILL. Wow.

A moment. DEREK *starts clearing plates up.*

Stop it, Derek!

DAVID. You're not his boss.

JILL. *You're* not his boss, you just fucking sacked him.

Pause.

DAVID. I'm fucking sorry, okay.

Pause.

MANI (*carefully*). I know we all think that we're great people
for having a disabled friend. That we're kind and patient
and understanding because we hold his drinks or ask him to
repeat himself. But I think maybe there's more complicated
difficult stuff, like this, that is part of David being disabled
too. And I guess maybe we have to make allowances for that
too.

JILL. I think you walked through a door marked 'woke' and came out through one marked 'loony bin'.

MANI. You shouldn't say loony bin. (*Beat.*) That was a joke.

JILL. I wouldn't quit the day job.

MANI. No, but... I mean, if I've learnt one thing about being disabled, I mean, it's probably what it does to your head.

DAVID *reacts physically.*

I'm not trying to be cruel. Sorry. But – I mean forget people being cunts on dating apps. Just, growing up being excluded from shit. People looking at you or avoiding looking at you. School, can you imagine? People panicking when you open your mouth just to speak. The terror of falling out with a friend because that friend might be the one you have to rely on to feed you a fucking meal tomorrow. Sitting at home while your mates are out dancing. Not knowing when you can go for a piss. People talking past you, or for you. Having to manipulate people into doing what should probably be basic kindnesses because you're tired of straightforward begging. Having to plan everything. Not being able to just fancy someone a bit without wondering if they might just be the person to finally be there for you, all the time, forever. That's all got to do something. That's got to make you go a bit...

JILL. Loony.

MANI. Maybe sometimes you'd just go fuck it all, fuck everyone. Self-destruct. And then you have to claw yourself back up and say sorry, cos you mean it and also cos fuck knows you can't actually afford to lose people. I dunno.

DAVID *is crying.* LIAM *puts an arm round his shoulder.*

Sorry.

DAVID *shakes his head, he's not angry.*

JILL. Mani, I hear you. I just think getting it on with your mate's boyfriend...

DAVID. I'm sorry.

JILL. Right, well.

> JILL *goes. They let her. We hear the door shut, far away.*
> DEREK *stacks up some dishes and takes them off into the*
> *flat.*

MANI. Bit of drama.

> *Pause.*

DAVID. I'm really sorry about the gig.

MANI. It's because of you I started doing it again, you know?
(*Little pause.*) Has Derek got any cigarettes?

DAVID. He stopped.

MANI. Fuck's sake. Not everyone can stop. The system doesn't
work if everyone stops.

LIAM. I've got some.

DAVID. You don't smoke.

LIAM. I know. Not much. I don't with other people.

MANI. You're an antisocial smoker.

> LIAM *chuckles.*

DAVID. That's actually quite weird.

LIAM. Are you calling *my* behaviour weird?

> DAVID *shakes his head.*

MANI. Should I have gone after her?

DAVID. I should have.

> LIAM *offers* MANI *a cigarette.*

MANI. Nah you're alright. I'll help Derek.

> MANI *goes into the flat.* LIAM *puts the cigarettes away.*

DAVID. You can have one.

LIAM. Nah.

DAVID. If you want one.

LIAM. I do want one, I just. Dunno. In front of you. (*Beat.*)
    She's quite fiery, isn't she.

DAVID. Would you describe a man like that?

LIAM. Jesus, you can't say anything around you lot.

> *Pause. He lights a cigarette. Pats and lightly rubs* DAVID*'s
> forearm.*

DAVID. Do you hate me?

LIAM. You're not boring, are you.

DAVID. Don't know.

LIAM. You're a fucking car crash. Is that offensive?

DAVID. No.

LIAM. You make me want to stick around and see what
    happens. (*Pause.*) Do you think Mani's comedy's any good?

DAVID. Yeah I think he's brilliant.

LIAM. I could go with you next time.

DAVID. Will you turn up?

LIAM. Firm promise.

> LIAM *takes his hand from* DAVID*'s forearm, and leans
> forward to look at the arm.*

You've got spunk on you.

> DAVID *reacts slightly.*

Did you get a shower this morning?

DAVID. Yeah.

LIAM. It's from today then.

DAVID. I had a shower afterwards too. I must have missed a bit.

LIAM. A bit?! There's a whole streaky scab of it. It's like a
    snake shedding its skin.

DAVID *laughs*

You knew you were seeing me today.

DAVID. Did you have a wank today?

LIAM. I wouldn't have shagged someone.

DAVID. I didn't shag anyone. It was just a wank. I'd have been horrible company tonight if I hadn't. My speech was terrible.

LIAM. I might have been just a wank when I first came over

DAVID. You were hot.

LIAM. Fuck off with that.

DAVID. He wasn't even average.

LIAM. That's not better. It's worse. It's gross. (beat) Anyway, if some really hot guy had offered to come over and wank you off you wouldn't have said "no you're too hot, Liam's coming over later" would you?

DAVID. How often do you think hot guys want to meet me? When I go on Grindr it's not like when Beyoncé tickets go on sale. Can you do something for me?

LIAM. I'm not going to wank you off.

DAVID. I don't need you to. A pensioner is coming over in half an hour.

LIAM. A pensioner? Wouldn't surprise me.

LIAM *laughs in spite of himself.*

What is it, what do you want?

DAVID. Can you think properly about whether you're actually bothered by someone wanking me off earlier.

LIAM. You are so patronising. Do you know that?

DAVID. Yeah, it's because I'm clever and frustrated.

LIAM *thinks*.

LIAM. I guess no I don't mind. Not so much.

DAVID. Thank you.

A moment. Then LIAM *smiles/chuckles to himself.*

LIAM. There's no compromise with you, is there.

DAVID. I spend my whole life compromising.

LIAM. Jesus, wait there.

LIAM goes into the house.

DAVID. Where are you going?

LIAM (*off*). Wait there.

LIAM emerges again with a tea towel that he's wet the end of. He goes to DAVID *and uses it to wipe the dried spunk off* DAVID*'s wrist.* DAVID *puts the cloth down.*

DAVID. Can I ask you something.

LIAM. No. Just have a normal conversation.

DAVID. You know earlier when you said 'it wasn't a date'.

LIAM. When?

DAVID. About the day you didn't come to the station. Why did you say that?

LIAM. It wasn't a date.

DAVID. But why did you need to *say* it.

LIAM. Because it was inaccurate.

DAVID. It wasn't very inaccurate but that's not the question I'm asking you.

LIAM doesn't know how to answer this.

Can you fucking answer then.

Pause.

LIAM. I wanted to be friends with you. (*Pause.*) I wanted to have sex with you. I just…

DAVID suddenly starts crying.

Oh man. Don't. David. David. Sorry.

DAVID. It's not you. It's just always going to be that way.

LIAM. Course it's not.

DAVID. You don't know that.

He calms a bit.

It's why it's mainly partnered guys who want to meet me.
They know I can't expect anything more from them.

LIAM. We're gay. We're not like… There's no biological reason
why we have to have boyfriends or husbands or fucking
partners.

LIAM *gets on his feet but doesn't really know what to do now
that he's done so.*

I'm sorry I gave up. I thought you might not want to hear
from me.

DAVID. I'm sorry too.

LIAM. I'm not scared because of… this. (*He taps* DAVID*'s
wheelchair.*) I'm scared of you because you dig into me
and don't give up. I'm scared of you because you make me
realise, not that I'm a bit broken, but that I should probably
do something to fix myself. That's scary. (*Beat.*) And in spite
of that, in spite of every conversation with you being like a
fucking therapy session, when it comes down to it you think
you're the only person with any sort of issues. You only like
me because you think I'm hot.

DAVID. No I don't.

LIAM. Look at your friends. I'm not like Mani. I'm not your
kind of person. What if I'm just proof that you can have…
whatever you think someone like me is on your arm. (*Pause.*)
Say something. Normally you don't shut up.

Pause.

DAVID. I don't need a boy to be everything to me. I will always
have friends.

LIAM. You might not if you keep shagging their boyfriends.

DAVID *laughs.*

DAVID. One person can't be *everything* to someone.

LIAM. I'd be a total compromise.

DAVID. No. Do you remember what I said about looking at a bird and wishing you could fly? And how you just accept that you can't because you haven't got wings. I actually think you're brilliant. (Beat.) How many people do you see out there in the world that you can't ever imagine fancying or falling in love with? People on the street you barely notice, or who look so mad they make you laugh. Boring people you get stuck with at parties. But they're all out there, having sex and having people fall in love with them. And those people who love them, or fuck them, they're not thinking 'this is a compromise' just because they're not spending Christmas with Zendaya or Justin Trudeau.

LIAM. Who?

DAVID. Pretend I said Marcus Rashford.

LIAM. You fancy Marcus Rashford?

DAVID. Obviously. (*Beat*.) I can't believe I've slept with you but I don't feel like I don't deserve to. And I think I can maybe help you be happy. (*Beat*.) And I think the reason you might let me do that is that I'm broken too.

LIAM. One day I wouldn't be enough for you.

DAVID. One day you would want to be with someone you can climb a mountain with. That's okay. I don't want to marry you. I would like to casually date you and if we did I would just like you to admit we were casually dating. (*Pause*.) I'm sorry I haven't taken your problems seriously. I'm good at asking about things that are personal and hard, but I'm bad at actually allowing for them, and that's shit and I will work hard to get better at it.

LIAM *leans into* DAVID *and kisses him. It's a long kiss. It's special. When they stop there's a moment of quiet.*

LIAM. Phone Jill.

DAVID. She won't answer. (*Beat*.) I'm horrible on the phone.

LIAM. Try anyway. If she doesn't answer, go round tomorrow. Go to her plant shop.

DAVID. She'll be angry if I do that.

LIAM. Tell her you were made to by a guy you're casually dating.

They're both a bit startled by that. A kiss.

DAVID. This is actually incredible.

LIAM. Calm down. I'm just saying – I'm just saying that if we go somewhere like for a drink or a film then we can call it a date.

DAVID. And you won't be embarrassed?

LIAM. No.

DAVID. What a fucking abominable and fantastic evening. What are we going to do about my wanking?

LIAM. What?

DAVID. My wanking. What if things develop between us.

LIAM. Can we not jump the gun.

DAVID. I would want sex to be special with you.

LIAM. It will be special.

DAVID. I don't want you to have to wank me off and then worry that it was a mediocre sexual experience when all I needed it to be in the first place was a reasonable wank. I don't want you to feel like you have to jerk me off like a bored housewife.

LIAM. Fucking hell. Could we worry about that later?!

DAVID. Yeah.

LIAM. Sounds like you've had a bit of a rough patch.

DAVID. Yeah.

LIAM. Derek said something about you moving home.

DAVID. Can you imagine? It would be like death.

LIAM. Phone Jill. Text her.

DAVID. I will.

LIAM. Don't make excuses.

He places David's phone within his reach so he can type on it.

Just say sorry. (*Beat.*) Is her boyfriend hot?

DAVID. Yeah he's quite hot. Let's do this inside. I need to tell Derek I haven't sacked him.

They go inside.

The End.

A Nick Hern Book

Animal first published in Great Britain as a paperback original in 2023 by Nick Hern Books Limited, The Glasshouse, 49a Goldhawk Road, London W12 8QP, in association with the Hope Mill Theatre and Park Theatre

Animal copyright © 2023 Jon Bradfield and Joshua Hepple

Jon Bradfield and Joshua Hepple have asserted their rights to be identified as the authors of this work

Cover photography by Piers Foley, artwork by Studio Doug

Emoji set: rawpixel.com/Freepik

Designed and typeset by Nick Hern Books, London
Printed in Great Britain by Mimeo Ltd, Huntingdon, Cambridgeshire PE29 6XX

A CIP catalogue record for this book is available from the British Library

ISBN 978 1 83904 144 0

Woodland
CARBON
www.woodlandcarbon.co.uk
NICK HERN BOOKS
Printed on Carbon Captured paper

www.nickhernbooks.co.uk

facebook.com/nickhernbooks

twitter.com/nickhernbooks